Fearless Fighter

Fearless Fighter

An Autobiography

Vera Mlangazua Chirwa

Zed Books
LONDON & NEW YORK

In association with

and

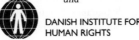

DANISH INSTITUTE FOR
HUMAN RIGHTS

Fearless Fighter: An Autobiography was first published in 2007 by Zed Books
Ltd, 7 Cynthia Street, London N1 9JF, UK and
Room 400, 175 Fifth Avenue, New York, NY 10010, USA
www.zedbooks.co.uk

Published in association with

Amnesty
International

and

DANISH INSTITUTE FOR
HUMAN RIGHTS

The Danish Institute for Human Rights' contribution to this publication
was funded by the Royal Danish Ministry of Foreign Affairs

Designed and typeset in Cumbria, UK, by Long House Publishing Services
Cover design by Andrew Corbett
Printed and bound in Malta by Gutenberg Press Ltd

Distributed in the USA exclusively by Palgrave Macmillan,
175 Fifth Avenue, New York, 10010, USA

A catalogue record for this book is available from the British Library
Library of Congress Cataloging-in-Publication Data is available

ISBN 978 1 84277 965 1 hb
ISBN 978 1 84277 966 8 pb

Disclaimer: The publisher has been unable to contact the copyright holder
of some photographs. If notified we will be pleased to rectify
any errors or omissions at the earliest opportunity.

To my dear Husband Orton Edgar Ching'oli Chirwa QC,
For making me what I am,

To my children,
Who loved me through being too hurt to love and encouraged me
to write this autobiography,

To Amnesty International for fighting for my release from prison
from day one of our unlawful imprisonment,

To all those who have rendered support of any kind for this book
to be published

Contents

Acknowledgements

Fearless Fighter came about as a result of the dedication and commitment of the Danish Institute for Human Rights (DIHR). It was
a collaborative project and would not have been possible without
the help of many people.

The initial concept for the book was developed by Vera Chirwa
and Kirsten Lund Larsen, and its realisation is a result of the work
and enthusiasm of Birgit Lindsnæs, Tomas Martin and Klaus
Slavensky at the DIHR. Kirsten Lund Larsen and Tomas Martin
interviewed Vera Chirwa for the book. Tomas Martin took down
the story and wrote up the material, which he co-edited with
Kirsten Lund Larsen. Tomas Martin also carried out photo
research and editing. Mette Holm and Thomas Trier Hansen sub-
edited the manuscript, and technical support was provided by
Anne Louise Piel Christensen and Brendan John Sweeney.

Everyone involved in the project is indebted to Professor Kings
Phiri for his detailed knowledge of and advice on the history of
Malawi. The project is also indebted to the colleagues and friends
of Orton and Vera Chirwa and to Malawian scholars and activists,
who have offered their comments and given perspective to the
story. A special thanks from Vera Chirwa to Nyamazao Marjorie
Mshana, Professor David Rubadiri, Kathryn English, late Ivy
Chipofya-Mshali (may her soul rest in peace), Alison and Colin
Cameron, and Amnesty International. Thanks are also due to The
Society of Malawi, the Malawian *Daily Times* and *Nation* newspapers, Kirsten Lund Larsen and Vera Chirwa for their permission
to reprint the photographs included here.

Foreword

Malcolm Smart

AMNESTY INTERNATIONAL

When Vera Chirwa, her husband Orton and their grown-up son Fumbani left the small Zambian town of Chipata on Christmas Eve 1981 they were embarking on a journey that was to change all of their lives. They expected to attend a meeting with other Malawians who supported their efforts to promote democracy in Malawi but instead fell into the hands of the Malawi authorities. Even now, the circumstances remain unclear but it appears that they were the victims of a plot orchestrated by security officials loyal to Malawi's then Life President, Dr Hastings Kamuzu Banda.

They were forced to stop, then seized and abducted by armed men who took them across the border into Malawi. There, after more than six months in detention, Orton and Vera Chirwa were put on trial for their lives, accused of plotting the violent over-throw of President Banda. Their trial was conducted before a so-called Traditional Court and was unfair. They were not allowed defence lawyers and their requests to call certain witnesses from abroad to testify on their behalf were denied by the Traditional Court's judges – a panel of five traditional chiefs who were not required to have any formal legal training. Unsurprisingly in these circumstances, in May 1983 Orton and Vera Chirwa were convicted and sentenced to death. The case then went to Malawi's National Traditional Court of Appeal, where the outcome was the same even though the Appeal Court acknowledged that there had been serious deficiencies in the trial and that the couple had been subject to 'unnecessary abuse'.

By this time, thanks to the efforts of the Chirwas' many friends and admirers, Amnesty International and others, their case had become something of a *cause célèbre* internationally, as well as in Malawi, and many people were mobilised in their support. Several African heads of state as well as Western governments and the United Nations appealed directly to President Banda to spare their lives and, ultimately, in June 1984 he bowed to this pressure, announcing that their sentences had been commuted to life imprisonment. In the meantime, after many months in which he was detained without charge or trial and held incommunicado, Fumbani Chirwa was released and allowed to leave the country. His release was greeted with particular relief because of earlier rumours suggesting that he had died in detention.

Tragically, although he escaped the hangman, Orton Chirwa was never to taste freedom again. He and Vera continued to be imprisoned, but kept apart, serving life sentences. According to reports at the time, Orton Chirwa was subjected to especially harsh conditions, being chained for long periods in his prison cell. In October 1992 he died at Zomba prison in circumstances that many considered suspicious.

Vera Chirwa, however, survived her ordeal and was eventually released in January 1993. By this time, Malawi was already undergoing a process of change. President Banda, once seemingly in total command of the country and its resources, was a reduced figure, age-ridden and on his way out of power. A new breed of younger politicians was finally coming to the fore and the pressures for change were becoming inexorable. It was into this 'new world' that Vera Chirwa stepped, free at last, ready to carry forward her ideals and commit herself to forcing those in power to have greater respect for the rights of all of Malawi's people.

Malawi had achieved independence in 1964 when Britain finally relinquished its protectorate over Nyasaland, as the country was formerly called. The path to independence had been a rocky one. For a time, Nyasaland had formed part of a federation with the two Rhodesias, now Zambia and Zimbabwe, in which political and economic power was monopolised by the white settler population based in Southern Rhodesia. The federation was ruled from Salisbury (now Harare), the Southern Rhodesian capital, by a white government although black Africans comprised the overwhelming majority of the population. Most of the wealth was also in white hands. Nyasaland was by far the poorest of the three territories, lacking the rich mineral resources of the two Rhodesias, and had the smallest white population, mostly grouped around the tea estates and plantations of its southern region. Essentially, Nyasaland was the unskilled labour pool for the federation and, indeed, beyond, with young men travelling each year to labour in South Africa's dangerous gold mines.

As a boy, Hastings Banda had also taken the long walk south to the goldfields, but he had been fortunate as well as determined, and later had been able to make his way to America. There, he studied and qualified as a medical doctor before moving to England and establishing himself as a general practitioner. From there, while continuing to work as a doctor, he became engaged with the African nationalist movement emerging back home. In Nyasaland and in the two Rhodesias, black leaders increasingly were calling for an end to racial discrimination and for equality and majority rule, and seeking to mobilise their followers in support of these demands. In Nyasaland, young and well-educated blacks led the charge, including Orton Chirwa, by then his country's leading black lawyer, and the charismatic Henry Chipembere and Kanyama Chiume. They recognised, however, that their very youth was an obstacle to effective popular mobilisation and so cast about to find an older, more experienced figure whose standing and prestige could galvanise support in the towns and villages, among the influential chiefs and village elders who would dismiss them as upstarts. Dr Hastings Kamuzu Banda was the man they chose. They persuaded him to give up his English medical practice and return home, warning him that he should be prepared to be greeted as a 'messiah'.

Back in Africa, Banda rapidly became the undisputed leader of the nationalist movement in Malawi alongside Kenneth Kaunda and others in Northern and Southern Rhodesia. Alarmed, the white settler-dominated federal government resorted to repressive measures, taking emergency powers and detaining African nationalist leaders, but this merely inflamed passions and demands for majority rule. In Britain, public attitudes were shifting, too: it became increasingly clear that in a changing world the pattern of colonial empire that had existed before the Second World War was no longer sustainable. British Prime Minister Harold Macmillan signalled this policy about-turn in a memorable and brave speech delivered to a packed (and hostile) Afrikaner-dominated whites-only South African Parliament. The 'winds of change' were blowing through Africa, he warned, and the British government preferred to go with the wind rather than try to stand against it. This was too bitter a pill for the Afrikaner nationalist government in South Africa, which left the Commonwealth and became a republic, but it marked a sea-change in Central Africa.

Dr Banda and other African nationalist leaders were released from detention and rapidly ushered into power in Nyasaland and Northern Rhodesia – though not in Southern Rhodesia, where the British government shied away from confronting the much stronger and more strident white settler community. After an initial period of 'responsible self-government' in which African nationalist leaders ruled with the support of the British colonial power, both Nyasaland and Northern Rhodesia gained their independence from Britain in 1964 as Malawi and Zambia respectively.

In Malawi, the euphoria that accompanied independence did not last long. Six weeks in, long-brewing differences between Dr Banda and his younger cohorts finally burst into the open. A dispute arose as to whether the new state should accept assistance from the Communist government in China, as Chipembere and the other 'young Turks' advocated. Banda declared this unacceptable and accused Chipembere of undermining his authority, causing a major Cabinet split from which Banda emerged supreme. Having already cemented his support among traditional chiefs and within the ruling party, he manoeuvred adroitly to isolate his younger critics and drive them from power. Orton Chirwa, who had become Justice Minister at independence, sided with the Prime Minister's critics and left the government. Subsequently, he and Vera left the country and went into exile abroad. They were not to return until that fateful Christmas Eve night in 1981.

Following the Cabinet split, Dr Banda moved quickly to consolidate his power. He put down an attempted insurrection led by Chipembere in 1965 and two years later an armed incursion by another of the ousted Cabinet ministers, Yatuta Chisiza. He also fostered the development of the Young Pioneers, a powerful youth organization and instrument of political control and enforcement in the streets and countryside. Patrolling the towns and villages, the Young Pioneers were allowed to act as a law unto themselves, preying on the public and targeting individuals and communities considered to be disloyal or disrespectful to the President – particularly Jehovah's Witnesses because of their refusal, for religious reasons, to join the ruling Malawi Congress Party (MCP) or to buy MCP membership cards. The following years of Banda's rule were punctuated by successive waves of attacks on Jehovah's Witnesses and many Witnesses were imprisoned.

In 1966, two years after independence, the constitution was changed to make Malawi a republic and a one-party state, and Dr Banda became President. Five years later, as if to emphasise the unassailability of his power, he made himself Life President of Malawi. Increasingly, he displayed a marked intolerance of criticism and an insistence that any and all achievements should be attributed to his wise and fatherly rule. Censorship was strictly enforced, networks of informers were promoted and anyone heard to make remarks considered critical of the President was liable to arrest and detention.

Unlike the leaders of other newly independent African states such as Tanzania and Zambia, Banda looked to the apartheid government in South Africa for economic, diplomatic and, when necessary, military support. Malawi became the first African state to open diplomatic relations with South Africa and Banda became the first African head of state to make an official visit to South Africa.

By the early 1970s, Malawi was caught in the grip of repression and several hundred people were detained without trial. In October 1975, Amnesty International reported that there were some 700 political detainees in Malawi, including suspected supporters of the former Cabinet ministers, civil servants who had fallen into official disfavour, academics, journalists and teachers who were considered suspect, and Jehovah's Witnesses. Detainee numbers continued to climb until late 1976, when a programme of mass releases began following the arrest of two senior officials in October: Albert Muwalo Nqumayo, who prior to his arrest had appeared to be Banda's most powerful government minister, and Focus Martin Gwede, head of the security police. They were charged with treason, tried and convicted by a Traditional Court, and in February 1977 sentenced to death. Gwede's sentence was later commuted, but Muwalo was hanged in September 1977.

Following the fall of Muwalo and Gwede, an estimated 2,000 political detainees were released in batches. Many gave grim accounts of the conditions to which they had been subjected at Mikuyu detention centre, where the majority had been held, and at Zomba prison. Those freed included the trade union leader Chakufwa Chihana, later to become a political party leader and presidential candidate in Malawi, and journalist Victor Ndovi, whose four years in detention arose from a report that he had filed for the BBC. Despite the releases, there was no significant shift in the pattern of repression, and new arrests and detentions continued to be reported in the succeeding years despite the high level of official secrecy surrounding such events. Yet more senior figures fell from grace in 1980, when Gwanda Chakuamba Phiri, responsible for the feared Young Pioneers, and Aleke Banda, who managed an important company which Dr Banda was rumoured to have used for personal enrichment, were detained. Both men remained in prison for several years.

By the early 1990s, the political situation in southern Africa had been transformed. African nationalist governments had entrenched their rule in Mozambique and Zimbabwe and at last the winds of change could be seen to be blowing inexorably in South Africa and Namibia, the last bastions of white minority rule. As a process of democratisation swept the continent, Banda's idiosyncratic form of tyranny appeared increasingly outdated and an obstacle to Malawi's development. Internal criticism, so long suppressed, could no longer be contained. In March 1992 the country's Catholic bishops published a pastoral letter which challenged the regime head-on and sparked wider demands for political change. Bowing to the growing pressure, the following October Banda announced that a national referendum would be held to decide whether the ruling Malawi Congress Party should retain its monopoly of power or the country should return to a multi-party system in which opposition parties would be tolerated. The timing of this – as it turned out, momentous – announcement coincided almost precisely with Orton Chirwa's death in prison, prompting suspicion that there might be some direct link between the two events.

It was into this political maelstrom that Vera Chirwa, newly widowed, at last stepped free after 12 years in prison. Remarkably, she scarcely paused to take breath before plunging into the thick of political organization and debate. Turning down the offer of a well-paid position in Geneva, she accepted appointment as director of the Malawian Law Society's Legal Resource Centre and thereafter resumed her activism in support of women's rights, begun during the anti-colonial struggle. After founding and leading Women's Voice, she established Malawi CARER – the Malawi Centre for Advice, Research and Education on Rights – to raise awareness of and strengthen activism for human rights, so helping her country to emerge from the shadow of the Banda years. Her contribution to human rights has not been limited to Malawi, however. Appointed to the 11-member African Commission on Human and Peoples' Rights, her work in recent years has focused on carrying the message of human rights to other parts of the African continent; specifically, as the African Commission's Special Rapporteur on prisons she has sought to improve conditions for prison inmates, one of the most vulnerable groups in any African country.

Vera Chirwa's life takes in Malawi's pre-independence struggle, the vicissitudes of exile and then detention, trial and the shadow of the gallows, widowhood, and then the challenge to rebuild Malawi after the Banda years. Throughout, she has faced every obstacle, every threat, every setback with courage and determination, and with faith that what she is doing is right. She has done so, too, with a seeming lack of rancour or bitterness towards those who have opposed her or done her harm. She is a remarkable person, and hers is a remarkable story.

Malcolm Smart*
London, August 2007

* Malcolm Smart was Amnesty International's researcher on southern Africa, including Malawi, at the time of the Chirwas' arrest and trial. Amnesty International declared their trial grossly unfair and sent an international legal observer to the appeal hearing, but he was denied entry to the court by the Malawi authorities. Subsequently, Amnesty International mounted an international campaign against the death sentences and, after these were commuted, continued to press for the release of Orton and Vera Chirwa as prisoners of conscience.

1 *A Family of Politicians*

Vera Means Truth

That day I had decided to disobey.

'Go and get the plates', my grandmother said.

She was cooking. Both my parents were very strict. They brought us up to be obedient, god-fearing and helpful, but on this particular day in 1937 I told myself:

'Let me try to disobey and see what happens. Maybe God will come and do something to me.'

I was five years old and had never tried it before. So I said:

'No.'

My grandmother was shocked.

'No? The food is ready, now go and get the plates. You know where they are. You always do that!'

'No, I am not going to collect the plates', I said.

She got up, collected the plates from the house and prepared everything herself. I took the food to my parents, uncles and aunts as usual and came back to the kitchen where grandmother and I ate together. She did not want to upset the meal and wanted all of us to eat first.

After the meal I washed the dishes and we went to sit on the veranda with my parents.

'Do you know what Vera did today?' grandmother asked. 'I asked her to get the plates and she refused.'

'Come here, Vera', my father said. 'Is it true that you disobeyed your grandmother?'

I never lie. In secondary school, I wrote a letter to the Scottish doctor who delivered me, because I wanted to know the meaning of my name.

'Write to Dr Stewart', my father said and handed me the address. 'She is the one who gave you that name.'

I wrote to her, and she wrote back to tell me that Vera means truth. Things sort of fell into place then.

'That's why I love the truth', I told myself.

That evening on the veranda, I did not lie either, and my father sent me to the bush. I had seen my mother and father whipping my younger brothers with the branches of a certain tree, and I understood that I was supposed to go and pick some of them. I deliberately picked a large one, and my mother and father laughed.

'You want me to kill you?' my father said. 'Come on. Go and pick a proper whip. Bring me six.'

When I came back with the branches I had to take off my panties and he started whipping me. I did not know that a parent will stop whipping you when you cry. They then feel you have repented, but I was a proud girl and refused to cry. After breaking the second whip, my grandmother wanted him to stop, but he continued till all of them were broken.

'Pick everything up and throw it away in the bush', he told me, and I went into the bush with the six broken branches and a very swollen behind.

'They are never going to see me again. Let me be eaten by hyenas right here in the bush!' I told myself and walked away.

When darkness fell I came back and hid in my grandmother's maize field. I could hear them:

'Is Vera with you?'

'No, I thought she was over there with you. . . .'

They started to look for me and to quarrel. My grandmother was furious:

'This is not the way to discipline a child!'

'You are the one who told us that she had disobeyed', my parents argued. 'We don't want our child to disobey you or anyone else!'

They went to the neighbours asking for help and the whole village started to search for me. From my hiding place in the maize field, I could hear them blaming my parents:

'Are you fond of whipping children? You like that, hah? Now you've lost her. She's probably been eaten by a lion or a hyena by now.'

Around 10 p.m. I decided that I had taught them a lesson. I started to cough a bit and they found me.

'Oh, Vera, Vera, you have troubled your parents and your grandmother so much!'

But I was a quiet child and did not say a word that night. From that day on I did not disobey and they never beat me again.

It was a custom among our Ngoni tribe that the first-born child was taken to the paternal grandparents when it was weaned, in order not to interfere with the birth of younger siblings. I was born in 1932 as an eldest child and spent my early childhood with my grandparents. I really loved my grandfather. He was the first African to be ordained as a reverend in Nyasaland and was stationed in Loudon in the northern part of the country at the Embangweni Mission. My other grandfather was also a reverend in the neighbouring Ekwendeni Mission. I think my mother and father met through the social events that linked the two missions, and married in 1930. My grandfather, Jonathan Chirwa, travelled a lot to other mission stations to preach, and he always brought me local fruit or small things he had found on his journeys, and which he thought might interest a child. We were very fond of each other, but he died suddenly in 1936.

I remember quite vividly that I was sitting in the moonlight with my grandmother in her room, and people were wailing and crying.

'Your grandfather has gone to God. He has gone to Heaven', she told me.

Okay, I thought, but then something started to confuse me. In the evenings people used to sit outside around the fire and tell stories, and they would ask me:

'Vera, where's your grandfather?'

'Oh, my grandfather, he has gone to Heaven.' And to my surprise they would all laugh. It went on for some time and one day I asked my grandmother where he really was.

'God took him, my dear. He is now in Heaven and we'll go and meet him when we die.'

'Does that mean I am not going to see him again?' I asked.

'Not on this earth', she said and I finally realised that he had left me and started to cry.

The following day these people asked me again and I said:

'My grandfather will not be seen on this earth. He is with God and I am going to see him when I die', and they never asked me again.

To this day it bothers me that they made a joke out of my misery just because I could not understand where my beloved grandfather was. I was only four years old, but that kind of insensitivity has angered me ever since.

A Family of Politicians

When I was a child, we did not know what the inside of a European house looked like. The Europeans were like gods to us. If you went to see relatives, who were working for them, you could hardly enter the kitchen. But my mother, Elizabeth Chiwambo, stood up against all that. In the church at Ekwendeni Mission there were separate doors and benches for the Africans and the Europeans. There were only a few whites, among whom were Mr and Mrs Larkin, but they nevertheless had their own door. My mother was exceptionally well dressed for an African woman and carried herself in a European way, with hat, stockings and high heels. One day Mr Larkin summoned her after church. She could not enter his house and he confronted her on the veranda:

'Do you want to be like the European women? I see you are dressing up in church and doing your hair like a European. What are you up to?'

'What is your problem?' my mother asked, 'This is my body and I do my hair as I please. My husband buys me dresses and I can dress as I want.'

'Oh, you are being very rude, Elizabeth!' Mr Larkin said.

'No, you are being rude, questioning me like that!' my mother snapped back, and the missionaries soon marked her as a troublemaker who would 'spoil' other African women.

My father, Theodore Kadeng'ende Chirwa, had similar encounters. He was a medical officer in charge of Mzimba Hospital. He had undergone medical training at the mission in Livingstonia, was highly qualified, and had his own practice as a doctor, but his English colleagues did not like him. The British doctors posted in Mzimba were all very young and inexperienced. When they examined a patient together with my father, who was very skilled, they found it difficult to accept his opinion. The white doctor, for example, would prescribe a certain treatment or drug, and my father might say:

'No, this patient needs an operation right away or she will die!'

But a white man would not allow a black man to overrule his decision. Sometimes my father would give in and find the patient dead after a few days, but more often than not he would insist on his own diagnosis and challenge his white colleagues. He became increasingly unpopular.

After my grandfather passed away my mother and father and his two younger brothers came to live with us in Loudon, and as a child I often heard my parents talk about politics. My mother always pointed out the evils of colonial rule and in the end it made them leave the country. My father was offered a better job in Congo. He left first, but before my mother followed him her brother, MacKinley Chiwambo, was arrested.

He was a civil servant. African civil servants were educated and able to enlighten the people about colonial oppression, and the Europeans generally did not stop them from being politically active. However, uncle MacKinley was very active and a pioneering member of the Nyasaland African Congress executive committee and he was put in jail for inciting his people to seek self-rule. I have strong memories of going there with my mother to visit him. He was in a bad state. He was sleeping on the bare concrete floor and had wounds all over his body.

'Sister,' he said, 'although you are a woman I'll show you this so you can see how I am being tortured here.'

He pulled down his trousers and his genitals were badly hurt. It was terrible. We both dropped tears. We prayed for him and left. He was released one and a half years later and sent to a mosquito-infested village near Port Herald to rot. We exchanged letters while I was in Blantyre Secondary School.

'We are being oppressed', he wrote to me, 'and now I am suffering because I was trying to point out to our people that this is wrong. I hope you understand.' I understood quite well.

My other uncle on my father's side, whom I stayed with after my parents had left, was also politically conscious and progressive. He ate dinner at the table, had tea at four o'clock and took a stroll in the afternoon, all unheard-of activities for an African at that time. He was very critical of the European oppression of our people. He held the meetings of the local branch of Nyasaland African Congress in his house, and I listened to all their discussions. Even my grandparents, who were sincere Christians, would integrate criticism of the inequalities we were experiencing in their prayers and sermons; for as long as I can remember, my family of politicians has influenced me.

Love at First Sight

I went to stay with my uncle Walter Chiwambo in Livingstonia when my parents left for Congo. I really enjoyed school and I was exceptionally good at it, especially at arithmetic and maths. At that time girls were seldom encouraged to go to school, but my grandmother was remarkably open to the idea.

'If she wants to go to school, let her go to school', she said, and my parents sent the school fees from Congo.

In Livingstonia I was the only girl out of 72 pupils, and when I went to study for the Junior Certificate at Blantyre Secondary School, I was again a lonely girl among 24 boys. It did not go unnoticed when I was home for holidays. After church the local women would surround my grandmother and me:

'What is this education for women? The winner of the bread is the boy. Vera should learn to do domestic work. Why should she go to school? When is she going to get married?'

It was always like that and I did my best to sneak out of church by the side door right after service to avoid their weekly attack.

I wanted to become a doctor, but I could study no further in Blantyre. The school only had three teachers and pupils had to queue up for the final exam. I had to wait a full year and my father promised to find another school for me, maybe in Uganda or South Africa. But I could not wait at home with all those women nagging me! Luckily, Domasi Teacher's Training Centre opened a higher-grade teacher's course, and my parents sent me there to spend my time sensibly while they were looking for another school for me. That year Orton Chirwa had finished his BA and went to teach in Domasi.

Orton was 13 years older than me. He had finished his primary education in Livingstonia and had married, but he was very keen on continuing his education. His father had a clothing business in Northern Rhodesia and called Orton to go there and work for him. There was no secondary school in Nyasaland at that time and his parents thought all this education business was fruitless.

'You are going to take over this shop, son. You have to learn how to make clothes and settle down', his father told him, and in Africa you cannot disobey your parents.

Orton could not say no to his father and had to accept being placed in front of a sewing machine. But he just kept breaking the needles deliberately, claiming to be doing his best, until his frustrated father finally relieved him of this vocation. He then worked hard as a teacher and saved enough money to take his A levels by correspondence. He managed to get the Nyasaland government to sponsor his BA studies at Fort Hare University in South Africa, where he majored in philosophy and obtained a distinction. Orton's then father-in-law was displeased with Orton's long absence and advised his daughter, Emily Nyamuhoni, to divorce Orton. Orton's mother was subsequently charged with the upbringing of their three daughters by Chief Timbiri of Nkhata Bay.

In Domasi I was living with the family of the headmaster of the primary school, Mr Chongwe, who happened to be Orton's friend. Mr Chongwe had offered Orton a place to stay while he was looking for a house in Domasi. I was in the kitchen preparing food for the family when Orton arrived by car. He must have been one of the first Africans in Nyasaland to own one.

'Vera, come and help with the luggage', Mr Chongwe called, and then he introduced us: 'This is Vera Chirwa. She is here as a student. You are going to be her teacher.'

'Oh, I didn't know that there were such beautiful girls in Nyasaland', Orton said, and I blushed.

'No, no, no', said the humour-loving Mr Chongwe. 'This girl

Orton Edgard Ching'oli Chirwa, QC, called to the Bar in 1958

Courtesy of Vera Chirwa

is a Chirwa. She's your sister, Orton'.

'It can't be. My sister is in the village.' And they went on joking like that, while I took the suitcase to his room.

I had many offers. Men even wrote to me from Zambia proposing marriage, but I refused all of them. However, with this one, Orton Chirwa, it was love at first sight. I loved him and he loved me right there on the spot.

He moved into his own house and one day after class he invited me for a cup of tea. If he had lived alone, I would not have gone, but he was sharing a house with his friend, David Rubadiri, who was later to become Vice-Chancellor of the University of Malawi. I decided to accept the invitation, but did not dare tell Mrs Chongwe in case she might not allow me to go. We had tea. Rubadiri pretended that he had to leave and left Orton and me alone. Then he proposed to me and I duly refused. It is our custom that decent girls do not say yes too easily. It makes you look cheap. In the North we are taught that if you want to marry properly and keep your family name respected you have to test the men and make sure they do not take advantage of you. I said:

'No.'

'You know me,' Orton replied, 'I'm a proud man. No woman refuses me. So, is that the end of it?'

'Yes, that's the end of it', I said and went home.

He came back over the next three months and I refused him three times. In the meantime I was taking advice from friends and from my aunt Rose Chiwambo:

'Orton Chirwa, the only graduate in Nyasaland, is proposing to me. What do you think?'

They all encouraged me and said that Orton had a good character and was a modest man. I was also pleased by his manners and he did not smoke or drink. He seemed like a genuine man who would respect my family, and he was well built. Men were wearing shorts then and Orton had nice legs. And he was very active politically.

My awareness of the injustice grew stronger and stronger in my youth, and support for the NAC was rising dramatically around that time. The colonial government wanted to impose an amalgamation, as they called it, of Southern Rhodesia (which is now Zimbabwe), Northern Rhodesia (now Zambia) and Nyasaland (Malawi). The white settler communities in Southern and Northern Rhodesia pushed very hard for this amalgamation in order to build a strong settler state with Nyasaland as a kind of 'homeland' for Africans who would supply cheap labour for the mines and the estates of the Europeans. In reality, they wanted to build an apartheid system like South Africa's. The NAC saw through this and mobilised the people; their opposition was strong enough to force the British government to cancel its plans. However, before long they imposed a federation of the three states on us instead. They claimed it was a loose union of independent states, but in fact the settlers were sneaking their agenda in through the back door. Again the NAC rallied the people, this time against the federation. And now we demanded our freedom as well.

His education had equipped Orton to read the political manoeuvres of the colonial government clearly and he had been adopted as a member of the NAC executive committee. The government published a white paper on the background and consequences of the Federation and Orton was assigned by the NAC to digest it and inform the people what prospects the settlers' plans held for them.

The NAC arranged a massive meeting in Blantyre and we all went to listen to Orton. There was no proper platform, but he climbed on top of two tables and addressed us non-stop from 10 a.m. to 4 p.m., enabling people to understand what was going on and encouraging us to take a stand. I was impressed. He was immaculately dressed, handsome, full of humour and undoubtedly a born leader. That performance cemented our love. On the way back from the meeting we sat together in the front of the bus, flirting and totally forgetting that my uncles were sitting in the back.

When finally I accepted him, we went to see my father's younger brother, Crosby Chirwa, who was my guardian while my parents were in Congo. My uncle was tough on Orton:

'No! Our daughter wants to become a doctor. We are looking for a school for her. You are much older than her and more educated. How can we be sure of your respect for her and for us? You may be too proud and beat her, and we don't want any ill-treatment of Vera.'

I was in the kitchen with my aunt, who was comforting me:

'Don't you worry. Your uncle has already decided. He is just testing him. We don't want to say yes right away and make you look cheap. If he wants to play with you, your uncle will scare him away, but if he is serious he'll persist. Don't worry.'

After three days, my uncle agreed on the condition that Orton swore to take care of my education. We got married in 1951. I was 19 years old.

Immediately after our marriage, Orton ordered lectures for my O-level from the Joint Matriculation Board in South Africa and I was studying at home. Orton coached me on every subject – except maths, which he always claimed I was better at than him.

I was soon expecting our first child and I often fell asleep while reading. I have a photographic memory and although I had slept under a tree most of the day, I could cheat convincingly when Orton was testing me in the evening. I passed.

The Colour Bar

Racism was ubiquitous then. We called it 'the colour bar'. There was a clerk called Milner at the Public Works Department in Domasi, where we stayed right after our marriage. Milner's office was close to the Teachers Training Centre, where Orton was still teaching. In order to show that even an educated African was nothing as far as a European was concerned, Milner deliberately humiliated Orton in front of his students:

'Come here, Chirwa, and carry this typewriter to my office.' And Orton would carry it, fuming with anger. Milner was not an educated man, but he was white.

'Look what this Milner is doing to me in front of my own students', Orton complained when he got home. 'Now, my dear, I want to be free and I am not going to be oppressed by anybody. I am leaving this job right now. I think I should become a lawyer.' I supported him all the way.

The colonial government had promised to support his Master's degree, but they did not welcome the idea of having an African lawyer in Nyasaland.

'You are going to fail', they told him. 'Even Europeans are failing the bar exam. It is very difficult. An African will not pass.'

'If they fail it's because they are stupid', Orton insisted. 'I'm an intelligent man. I'm going to pass.'

He went to London to study law in 1956. With Orton gone I had to take care of the three children and managed to get a job as a clerk in the Ministry of Lands in Zomba. I was the only African and the only woman working there. A young man from Southern Rhodesia was employed shortly after me. He was less qualified and we performed exactly the same tasks, but it turned out that I was only paid three quarters of his salary. I complained, and they told me quite frankly that it was because I was a woman. I told them it was unfair since I, as opposed to my male colleague, had children to take care of. They tried to compensate by promising me a room in the government hostel nearby, but it was solely occupied by European women, spinsters and daughters of the heads of department, who did not want a young African mother with three children as their neighbour. Instead, I had to rent a house about five miles into the hills between Zomba and Domasi.

Our third child, Fumbani, was only eight or nine months old and I was still breast-feeding him. The bus going to Zomba was slow and unreliable and I had to buy a bicycle. I used to wean my children according to a fixed system of introducing solids little by little at intervals of two, then three and four hours. It took time and was quite impossible in Fumbani's case. I could only feed him early in the morning and when I came home late in the evening, and I had to wean him by force. It bothered me and the resentment towards my employer was building from the start. The house we lived in was full of mosquitoes and the children were constantly suffering from malaria. Countless times I had to put all of them on the bicycle, Nyamazao on the saddle, Virginia on the handle-bars, and Fumbani tied on my back, and take them to the hospital. It was not easy.

I worked there for three years and the blatant racism and injustice I witnessed from my desk fuelled my political activism. Important and highly respected African officials, chiefs and politicians were simply referred to as boys, and senior African civil servants were receiving five or six times less payment than young white daughters of colonial officers, who were merely doing temporary holiday jobs while visiting their fathers. The examples were numerous and the last straw was when they refused to give me my hard-earned benefits.

Orton was also struggling in London. The government had refused him his scholarship mid-way and he had to support himself and pay his fees by working as a teacher. He really wanted to qualify as a barrister and get back home, and I decided to try and help him the best I could. My mother had taught me to knit stockings, cardigans and sweaters, and I tried to knit in my little free time and sell the things at work. It went very well and I ended up doubling my income through the knitting. Two months before Orton's final exam, I sent him my entire savings and told him to quit his piecemeal jobs, concentrate fully on his studies and get back to his family as quickly as possible. He wrote his exams and passed.

When he returned he immediately established the first non-European law practice in Nyasaland with an Asian lawyer, Mr Sakarani; they called it 'Chirwa and Company'. He had to wait three months to be admitted to the local bar and was living with me. In those days it was quite humiliating for a man to be maintained by his wife, but Orton and I were different in that respect and we did not mind. I asked for a paid holiday, to which I was fully entitled after three years employment, but they refused on the pretext that I was only temporarily employed. It was not true and this final act of ill-concealed discrimination made me resign immediately. They tried to persuade me to stay and when that did not work they demanded that I return one month's salary because I had resigned without notice. But I was prepared for this last ploy.

'Here's your money, I'm resigning today!'

The head of the department reported to the Chief Secretary, who was second only to the Governor, and the Deputy Chief Secretary called me to his office. It was the first time I had entered the office of one of the 'big people', as we called them.

'We'll give you all your benefits', he started, but I stood firm.

'You can keep your benefits. There is too much colour bar here. I have suffered too much and too long. I've made up my mind.'

They did not quite believe me and kept saying:

'Bye-bye, Mrs Chirwa. See you on Monday.' But they did not see me again.

Around that time the colonial government was pressing, persuading and inveigling the local chiefs to turn against the NAC and support the Federation. The very same day I resigned, Orton and I went to Mupemba to help influence the chiefs to go against the government, and I became a full-time independence activist.

2 Against an Apartheid Federation

The Lion Returns

Dr Hastings Kamuzu Banda had been a staunch supporter of the NAC's fight against the Federation. Dr Banda was originally from the central part of the country, but he left for South Africa as a young man to pursue a higher education. He got to the United States with the assistance of the African Methodist Church and managed to graduate as a medical doctor in 1937, as one of the first Malawians to get a degree. He went to England and started a practice, but he was very active in the anti-colonial struggle for his native country and sent funds and lobbied strongly for the NAC from London. When the Federation was declared in 1953, Dr Banda was quite disillusioned with the NAC and he toned down his political engagement. He left for Ghana to work as a medical doctor and that was where Kanyama Chiume and Henry Chipembere approached him in 1957.

Chiume and Chipembere were the foremost representatives of the young radical generation of the NAC, who had won the African seats in the Legislative Council in 1956. They were eloquent, educated and politically able, and they became very influential. I knew Chipembere from our schooldays in Blantyre Secondary School, where he was one year ahead of me. He showed his bravery even then, when he organised a student strike because of the lousy food we were given. He was a freedom fighter to the bone: a lovely, cheerful man who talked well and to the hearts of people, but also listened well. I loved him very much.

Chipembere, Chiume and the other younger NAC leaders wanted to escalate the struggle for independence. They were dissatisfied with some of the older members' tendency to work with rather than against the colonisers. But they were too young to take charge. They did not have the mileage to appeal to the masses as a national father figure would, and they were on the lookout for a strong leader who was as determined as themselves. They approached Dr Banda. He was reluctant at first, but agreed to return to Malawi and lead the NAC on one condition.

Chiume and Chipembere called an NAC executive meeting and presented the idea to us. Orton was still in Britain, but I attended the meeting as an NAC executive member. Some of us were not immediately impressed. Chipembere and Chiume talked highly of Dr Banda's virtues, but we did not know him and he had been out of the country for so long. Besides, we had an NAC president, T. D. T. Banda, who was still in office.

'Why can't Dr Banda come home, join the NAC and then stand for NAC president, when T. D. T. Banda's term expires?' we wanted to know.

'No, he wants to be president right away' Chiume said. 'Otherwise he will not come.'

They were very adamant and finally had their way.

Dr Banda arrived at Chileka Airport on 6 July 1958. Orton had returned from the UK just a few weeks earlier and we both went to the airport to greet our new leader. Orton, of course, had met Dr Banda in London and knew him well, but I saw him for the first time that day and he made a good impression on me. He was very determined and seemed genuine. And he could speak. His roaring voice burned through everything and he was soon nicknamed the 'Lion of Malawi'.

He also got his presidency. We wanted to strengthen our

organisation and turn it into a mass political movement, and the executive committee had asked Orton to draft a constitution for the NAC while he was away in Britain. With a lawyer's precision he had formulated a very modern draft based on the constitutions of political parties in the UK. He brought it to the NAC general conference in Nkhata Bay in August 1958, right after Dr Banda's return. At the end of the first day's session, Orton took the document out of his briefcase.

'It's time to discuss this', he suggested, but Chiume refused.

'Oh no, we are too exhausted. We need fresh heads for that decision. Let's wait till tomorrow.'

The following day, Orton tried again and was surprised to learn that another constitution had already been adopted. While Orton had been out, they had quickly passed a constitution designed to give Dr Banda absolute power over the organisation. Orton protested that the ultimate power should lie with the party itself, but it was too late. He had been 'couped', and it was not going to be the last time.

Dr Banda was elected president of the NAC and we all supported him, including Orton and me. T. D. T. Banda had been forced out. In a fierce confrontation, he had been accused of misappropriating funds and had to resign. Later on I was told by someone from the executive committee that foul play and false accusations had paved the way for our new leader.

The Dedza Massacre

Things were getting hot. The NAC had gained momentum with Dr Banda's return and the call for independence was now a storm sweeping up and down our narrow country. We all united behind Banda and campaigned tirelessly.

After quitting my job with the Ministry of Lands I began to

assist Orton as his secretary in court. I had always wanted to become a doctor, but it seemed quite impossible to leave my children for the seven years a medical education would take. Working with Orton was extremely interesting and I decided to become a lawyer instead. As the first African lawyer in Nyasaland Orton had begun to fill a huge gap in the administration of justice in our part of the world and I wanted to join him. This decision was obviously reinforced by the very apparent need to uphold the rule of law in the highly tense situation our country was in.

The white District Commissioners retorted harshly to the public demand for freedom and let us know that every 'troublemaker' would be convicted as charged – with or without evidence. Orton defended all our fellow NAC activists. They arrested 24 people for unlawful assembly and incitement of the public in Dedza, a Chewe district in the central part of the country, in January 1959, and Orton went to defend them. The trial took three days. The District Commissioner, Mr Davis, was a personal friend of ours, but he nevertheless insisted on convicting the 24 accused although there was no proper evidence against them. It really annoyed Orton, who said he would appeal any unjust ruling.

A large crowd had gathered around the courthouse to hear the judgement. We had been waiting for two days together with the mobile police force, which the white Magistrate had called to the scene. There was a primary school just beside the courthouse. It was around noon and the children were coming out from class just as the court officials left the building. There were people everywhere and it was tense. I noticed that the mobile police force had donned their helmets and that they were armed. It frightened me and I went over to the police commander.

'Why are you here? This is wrong. You can see that these people are quiet. They are not making trouble. And there are children all over the place. Do you want to provoke a situation?'

He just looked at me stone-faced. Then I saw the District Commissioner, Mr Davis, approaching with a megaphone, about to read out the Riot Act. I knew that when he had finished reading the Act the police would charge and beat people up. I ran straight up to him.

'Look Mr Davis, the children are leaving, but these NAC people will stay. You know that they are always here, singing their songs and demonstrating, but they do it in an orderly fashion. Please, stop the police.'

'There is nothing I can do. It is a government policy that these people have to disperse within three minutes.'

'Three minutes! How can you expect such a crowd to clear the area in three minutes?' I was furious and ran up and down between Mr Davis and the police commander: 'Dare you kill these people! We are going to see to you when we take over. We'll revenge these people. Dare you!'

As a lawyer Orton had to hold himself a bit aloof from the situation. While I was running around outside he was with his clients and the District Commissioner in the courthouse. He assured Mr Davis that the demonstrators would not make any trouble, and Mr Davis agreed to give us another five minutes.

Five minutes later they started shooting. Women with babies on their backs were running for their lives. Small children fell to the ground. People were shot dead. After the first round of firing most people had fled behind the corner of a big house and the police charged. We all ran to a nearby trading centre and the police just smashed everything in their path, chased people into the shops and stalls, and beat them up. Orton ran to our car, drove right up beside me and threw the door open.

'Jump in!' he yelled, but another man ran to the car, too. I had noticed him before, because he had been eagerly sabotaging my efforts to calm the demonstrators. Every time I urged the people to go back, he said: 'No, we have to stay, we have to stay', which confused people. It was a chaotic situation. I was hurt and we had to get away from there, and this man was hammering on the car.

'They are going to kill me! Help!', he cried.

We thought he was badly hurt and we let him into the car. As we drove off, we were talking heatedly about the massacre we had just witnessed. We were shocked and furious.

'How can they fire on people like that?' I asked. 'If we wanted to we could just as easily kill them.'

We drove past the huge mansions of the white people living beautifully up in the hills around Dedza.

'They just live up there, lonely and vulnerable. If we wanted to we could make a bloody uprising like the Mau Mau in Kenya. We could make a Mau Mau here, but we don't, and that's what we get in return!'

'Yah, let's kill them!' our passenger urged me.

This reference to the Mau Mau was later to form a fundamental part of a charge against me in a court case. I was put on trial for planning to kill white people. Actually it was the other way around. I was stressing that we, despite the suppression, held back, but that was not the prosecutor's opinion, and he claimed to have a reliable source. This source was of course the man to whom we unsuspectingly gave a lift. He reported everything back to the colonial police, and we later learned that he was a government agent planted among the demonstrators to escalate the conflict and give the police an excuse to fire.

State of Emergency

As the government tightened its grip, the NAC fought back with demonstrations and civil disobedience. Anxieties among the whites were aggravated by rumours and exaggerations in the press about whites being killed, beaten and raped. The whites worked themselves up into a fever pitch and began to talk of getting rid of 'the agitator Dr Banda' by assassination or other unlawful means. There were clear indications that the white community was about to take off the gloves. The NAC executive committee wanted to prepare the movement for the threat hanging over their leader's life, and they met in the famous 'bush conference' in February 1959. Opinions about what actually happened at the bush conference continue to differ. The government claimed that a massacre plot against the white community was planned at the meeting. Orton and I were not there, but it was obviously decided to intensify the struggle, including the throwing of stones against white people and their cars. One day on our way to Orton's office our car was stopped by a group of uniformed white settlers. The settlers had formed several armed militias, who were supposed to assist the police in restoring order, and they pulled us out of our car. Somebody had apparently thrown stones at them. We were among the very few Africans who owned a car and it confused them.

'I am a lawyer on my way to work', Orton said.

'No, we know you. You are the ones who are throwing stones. We are going to teach you a lesson!'

'How can a person in a car throw a stone?' Orton asked.

They took us to a nearby police station. We waited for hours together with many other detained Africans, but there were also a lot of white women and children around. They thought the Africans were about to kill every single white person in Nyasaland, and while the men were out harassing people on the streets the women and children sought refuge at the police station. It was a mess.

Eventually a senior police officer noticed Orton and was horrified to find the successful African lawyer, who had won all his cases against them, sitting among the other detainees.

'Sorry, Mr Chirwa. It was a mistake. These people are helping us out, but they don't know the procedures. Sorry for that.'

We were released and went home.

On 3 March 1959 there was a knock on our door at five o'clock in the morning. Secretary General of the NAC Dunduzu Chisiza, and two other executive committee members, Lali Lubani and Lawrence Makata, rushed in.

'Dr Banda has been arrested!'

'Why? What happened? What's the problem?' Orton asked.

'We don't know', Chisiza said.

'Don't worry. I'll bail him out', Orton assured them and they waited.

An hour later Governor Armitage was on the radio declaring a state of emergency under which NAC leaders were to be arrested and detained without trial. He argued that this step had been necessary to counter the mounting violence in the country initiated by the NAC, which, he claimed, had hatched a plot to massacre all prominent whites and their families in the country, including himself.

'I can't bail Dr Banda out in a state of emergency', Orton said, 'but I am going to find out where he is.'

The others were very upset. At 8 o'clock a search for our three visitors was announced on the radio. They were to surrender themselves on the spot or risk being shot.

'I won't run away. I won't run,' Chisiza said.

'You shouldn't', Orton cautioned him. 'All the borders are closed and alerted. They'll shoot you. Let me go and check what has happened to Dr Banda.'

Orton went to his leader's house and asked to see his client. He was put in an army car and taken to the airport. Dr Banda had been dragged out of bed and was still in his pyjamas.

'Oh, Chirwa. Very good! What can you do for me?'

'There is nothing I can do for you in a state of emergency, I'm afraid', Orton said. 'I would have bailed you out, but I'm sorry. I just insisted on seeing you and finding out where they had taken you.'

It was obvious that they were planning to fly him out of the country. Orton briefed him about his rights and emphasised that he was a detainee entitled to proper food and care.

'They are British. They know the law', was all Banda said.

Orton went home and from that day on the three NAC executives were hiding under our bed. Throughout the day their names were mentioned on the radio. They were wanted and anyone who harboured them would suffer the consequences. Orton warned me.

'Vera, you should be prepared for the worst.'

'It doesn't matter. We are dying for our country.'

'Don't you care about your children?' he asked.

'I do care, but what can we do? This struggle involves everybody.'

'Okay. I am prepared too. I just worry for you', he said.

Many people were coming to our house over the next couple of days asking for advice. International journalists also turned up on our doorstep, questioning Orton about the supposed massacre plot, which he dismissed as a lie. On the fourth night of the emergency, Orton sat down with the other executive members in his pyjamas.

'We are fighting for our freedom. What happens when the leader is gone? You replace him right away and continue the struggle. We form another executive committee and we are going to do that until they surrender.'

They wrote a new list of members for the NAC executive and elected Orton as their new president. We also agreed that it was too dangerous for Chisiza and the others to stay in our house. If the police had found them there they would have been killed, and they decided to give themselves up. Lali Lubani's house was less than a kilometre down the road and the next morning, just before dawn, the three of them hurried back through the forest. They called the police from Lubani's phone and were immediately arrested. The same afternoon our house was stormed.

The soldiers surrounded the house and pointed guns at us from every door and every window. They even pointed at the children, who started crying, but none of us could move. The beauty and uniqueness of Orton's and my relationship was that we told each other everything, so I knew about the list of the new NAC executive. I also knew that if they found it they would kill him on the spot.

'Where's the list', I whispered.

'It's here with me.'

'Give it to me now. Just do it quickly', and he passed it to me unnoticed as they started to search the house. I quickly put the list in my bra. They were on their walkie-talkies:

'Yes we got Orton Chirwa here. – No, not yet. – Not yet', they kept saying into the walkie-talkies as they went through our things, obviously looking for something specific.

Finally, they withdrew as suddenly as they had come. We all drew a deep, deep breath. It was close.

'You are a clever girl, my dear', Orton exclaimed and we rushed to comfort our three young children, who were totally distressed.

Orton started to sleep in his suit. We expected them to be back any minute, and we were not wrong. Three days later they were hammering on our door at 3 o'clock in the morning.

'We are arresting the lawyer Orton Chirwa. Open the door, please!'

'He's coming', I said. 'He's getting dressed.'

Orton had written out some post-dated cheques for me in case he was arrested. A lot of Rhodesian police officers had been brought in after the emergency and they were rumoured to steal from the people they arrested. I rushed to my sister-in-law's room. Orton's sister was staying with us, because she was bedridden with pneumonia. The Rhodesians might be thieves, but I did not expect them to drag a sick woman out of bed, and I made her lie on the cheques. Orton had gathered his things and I prepared myself to say goodbye to him.

'It seems you are going as well', Orton said.

'Me? I'm not a politician. I'm a housewife!'

The wife of a high-ranking police officer came to our bed-room: 'Yes, Mrs Chirwa, you are coming with us.'

'Why me? What have I done?'

'We don't know. It's just instructions', she said. She was a nice woman.

'But where am I going?'

'We don't know, but some of the other women who have been arrested have been sent to Rhodesia.'

'Rhodesia! Can I take some clothes?' I asked, a bit shaken.

'Yes, if I were you, I would take some', she said.

I found a small suitcase and started to pack a few things, clothes, creams and a beautiful little nail cutting set Orton had given me. They wreaked a lot of havoc in the house. We had just bought a brand-new lounge suite, which they cut up, looking for the famous massacre plot. They took all the papers and letters from the office room and were about to smash my new sewing machine.

'Wait, wait, wait!' I yelled and got the key for its cover from my bathrobe-pocket – no massacre-plot there either.

They led us out of the house. We left our children at 3 o'clock in the morning. I did not know whether they were awake or not.

'What is going to happen to our children?' I asked Orton. I wanted to turn around.

'Don't look back', he said. 'They are going to shoot you in the back and say you tried to run away.'

'Okay', I said and went into the army car that was waiting for us.

A Black Cat in Salisbury

They took us straight to Chileka Airport. At Chileka we met the Rubadiris, who had also been arrested. As well as sharing the house in Domasi with Orton when we first met, David Rubadiri had been best man at our wedding. He was a lecturer by then and politically active like the rest of us. His wife Gertrude is my cousin. For some reason they had handcuffed David.

Two English housewives were supposed to guard Gertrude and me and they escorted us to a separate room. We knew their husbands and had been to parties together and they were as disturbed by the situation as Gertrude and me.

'Why are we being arrested?' we asked.

'Oh, they say that the NAC people want to kill all Europeans in Nyasaland', they said.

'Oh really!'

'You don't know?'

'We don't know anything about that', we said.

'But you are members of the Congress, aren't you?'

'Yes, of course we are, but it's not true.'

'Ah, but we have seen one of them', they argued. 'These killers have decided not to cut their beards before every single European is slaughtered. We've seen one of them right here at the airport this morning.'

We had to laugh. They were referring to David, who was wearing a beard.

'But that's my husband', Gertrude said, 'It's just his style. He's not slaughtering anybody.'

We ended up joking with them and sharing a cup of tea together, but unfortunately they changed our guards. Two young Boers, a man and a woman, replaced our frightened English friends.

'You prisoners, get up!' the woman yelled and brutally searched us. She stole my nail-cutting set.

We were led to a military plane and were once again united with our husbands and a larger group of NAC members, who had been rounded up. They wanted to separate husbands and wives, but I looked quite young and they mistook another young lecturer, Vincent Gondwe, for my husband and ended up giving me a seat next to Orton. We took off and Orton briefed and supported me throughout the flight.

'You are not a criminal. You are a political prisoner, a detainee, and just like Dr Banda you have to insist on your rights – good food, beds, sheets, mattresses and so on. You have to be tough, my dear. This is how governments are won. When we come out the British are going to give us our freedom. And don't worry, the children are taken care of. God is there.'

When we reached Bulawayo the men got off the plane and were sent to Gwelo Prison, but Gertrude and I continued to Salisbury. The Boer guards left the plane with the men and some African guards, who were very sympathetic, took over. They gave us the latest news and told us horrific stories of how the Boers mistreated African prisoners. They wanted to give us some biscuits and oranges, but did not dare to go against their orders.

Institutionalised racism was spreading to Nyasaland due to the Federation, but we did not have the strict public segregation practised in Rhodesia. It was an apartheid regime we landed in, when we set foot in Salisbury, but they took us through the doors reserved for the whites because they did not want us to be seen by our fellow Africans. Finally, we reached Salisbury Prison and thanked God that they put us in the same cell.

The cell had two wooden frames lying on the floor, which were supposed to pass for beds. They gave us two narrow blankets, but still no food and for more than 24 hours we had nothing but the friendly cup of tea that the frightened white housewives had shared with us at the airport after our arrest. The following morning we were presented with a filthy plate of coarse, half-cooked *nzima* porridge. We were starving and had to hold our noses, purse our lips and try to suck up the porridge without touching the filthy edges of the plates. Both of us got severe diarrhoea for the next three days.

Our chief wardress was a very fat, white woman. I think she was terrified by the rumours about Africans plotting to kill all whites in Rhodesia and Nyasaland and felt that she had to be harsh on the two 'dangerous rebels' in her custody. To this day Gertrude and I can still joke about this frightened fat woman, who tried to play tough on us.

We were getting weaker by the day. I had some cash in my handbag and the fat woman agreed to buy us some fruit, biscuits and juice from the market outside. When she finally brought them she did not enter the cell but stood in the door yelling:

'When I come you must stand up!'

'If you hadn't eaten for three days, would you have the strength to get up from the floor?' I retorted. 'If we had a proper bed, I could maybe get up, but not from the floor.'

She threw everything straight at me and slammed the door. Luckily, I caught the glass bottles with orange juice.

We spent the next two months in that place. Some of the African wardresses were kind to us and deliberately packed our food in the latest newspapers. The food was awful, but we were grateful to satisfy our hunger for news when we unpacked our meals. The Prison Superintendent was ordered by the Governor to get statements from us about what we thought had contributed to the state of emergency. I think it was part of the inquiry of the

Devlin Commission, which was launched by the British government to look into the causes of public resistance to the Federation. We decided instead to write a long statement about the horrible conditions in the prison and were immediately called to the Superintendent's office.

'Why didn't you tell me?' he asked. 'I'm supposed to look after you and I'll be in serious trouble if something happens to you.'

'Ah, we already told this fat woman that we are detainees and should be treated accordingly, but she just laughs at us.'

It turned out that the fat woman was nothing less than the Superintendent's wife, but he just smiled and promised things would change. And it did change. His wife stopped tormenting us.

Reverend Doig, who was head of mission in the Presbyterian Church in Blantyre, also came to see us. Being British himself I suppose he managed to persuade the Governor to allow him to visit his church members. The reverend's visit occasioned quite a few improvements and we were moved to a new wing and allowed to do exercises in the courtyard. We told him everything – also that Gertrude was expecting. She must have been about three months pregnant by then and she was vomiting seriously.

One day, when we were doing our exercises, a black cat crossed the courtyard. I had heard that seeing a black cat like that was a bad omen and I was a bit disturbed. Gertrude insisted that it was a good sign and gave me a lot of examples of how she had experienced something good after seeing a black cat.

'Well, I don't know', I said, 'I have always thought it was a bad omen.'

Early next morning the fat woman and two other guards threw our door open. I thought of the cat and said to myself:

'They are going to kill us now. It's over.'

'You are going back home,' the fat woman yelled. 'Do you understand? Get your things. We are going to the airport now.'

Reverend Doig had gone straight to the Governor.

'Since when has it become an English practice to detain pregnant women? What is happening here?'

The Governor was apparently shocked to learn that one of his prisoners was pregnant and quickly arranged for Gertrude to be brought back to Nyasaland and placed under house arrest. They did not want to leave me behind and within hours we were back home in the country we were fighting for. From that day on I have always agreed with Gertrude. A black cat is a good omen.

Simama!

'Take off your panties!'

They had separated us right after we landed at Chileka Airport. Gertrude was escorted to her house by two policewomen, and I was put on a truck and taken to Zomba Prison. In Zomba I was searched by two white women. They must have been wives of the prison officers. I had to take off my clothes and bra and they ordered me to strip completely.

'I'm not going to take off my panties. Why are you searching me like this, when I'm coming straight from another prison? You whites just want to stare at African nakedness, but not with me, you don't! I don't want you to see me naked. If you want, you can start by taking off your own panties. Then it's okay. I see you, you see me.'

'Okay, Mrs Chirwa. Okay, okay, it's fine,' they said and let me go.

In Zomba I joined a group of five other women detainees, including my aunt Rose Chiwambo and another political activist and friend of ours, Mrs Ntenda, and her secretary. There were no cells for women and we were put in a makeshift shed. The men were close by. We could hear them cry out. And there was this noise:

'Bang!…Bang!…'

'What is that?' I asked Rose.

'Oh, Vera, people are dying here! They are beating them to death.'

'Really!' I could not believe that this was the sound we were hearing.

'Yah', Rose said, 'These Boers are beating our men up right now.'

We normally did not see many Boers in Nyasaland, but they had come from South Africa or Rhodesia as some sort of task force in connection with the emergency. There were three of them in the prison. One of them was really bad. We called him Simama, which is the Swahili word for 'stand up' that he always used. The prison officers had to pass through our shed to get into the men's area, and each time Simama went through we had to stand up. The first time I was quite surprised.

'Why are you standing?'

'No, Vera!' Rose said hurriedly, 'Stand up! You have to stand up!'

I got up and Simama walked slowly by, enjoying every bit of this show of deference. I did not like what I saw – Rose rushing to stand while she was busy breastfeeding her baby. We had to jump up even when we were eating. It was humiliating.

'Why all this standing?' I wanted to know.

'Don't start, Vera,' they all said. 'They are going to kill you. They kill people here, don't you understand. They have killed a lot already.'

'I see no reason why ladies should stand for men', I insisted.

We were sleeping on the bare brick floor and the food was close to inedible.

'I'm not going to eat this', I said.

'Vera, you're going to die.'

'My husband told me that we are not prisoners. We are detainees and we must eat good food like we eat at home and we should not sleep on bricks.'

After three days without food, I was getting weak. Rose tried to persuade me to eat, but I refused. I managed to get hold of pen and paper from one of the African guards and wrote a long letter to the prison's commanding officer about our mistreatment. We suspected that proper food was actually allotted to us only to be stolen by the guards. I put that down and turned their own arguments against them.

'If this is supposed to be a Federation,' I wrote, 'and this is a federal prison, the treatment we are given here should be the same as in Salisbury. There should be no differences in a federal system and I am demanding proper treatment, good food and a bed. We are made to stand up each time a prison officer is passing through. Why? In our culture ladies do not stand up for men. It is rather the other way around.'

The complaint really outraged Simama. He discovered I was writing something just as I was finishing the letter. I quickly signed the paper as he rushed over and snatched it from me.

'I'm going to tear this up', he said to the African guards after having read my complaint, but they cautioned him:

'These women are important people. You see how the white missionaries come to visit them. If you tear the note, sir, the missionaries will complain directly to the Governor.'

'Okay, I'll send it', he grumbled.

Later in the afternoon one of Simama's Boer colleagues came to our shed. Simama was bad, but this one was even worse. He abused us and made rude signs to our private parts.

'Come on, women', he yelled, and we had to get up. 'Today, you are going to have good food and proper beds to sleep in. But you little girl,' – he turned towards me – 'if you try to be clever with us, we'll be cleverer with you.'

'I still don't understand, why ladies are supposed to stand for men. Is it so in your culture?' I taunted him.

'There is no lady or Mrs here!' he yelled. 'You are prisoners!'

'No Mrs?' I snapped back, 'Are you going to dissolve our marriages?'

Rose got up and stood between the Boer and me: 'Vera, they can shoot you.'

'Let them. I don't care. I'm not going to be insulted.'

I won that battle and learned that they will always take advantage of a coward and always think twice if you are brave and courageous. Some beautiful, home-cooked food from the outside was brought to us within hours. And I was very hungry.

A week later the beds came, but they only brought two. By that time Mrs Ntenda and her secretary had been tried and put somewhere else, but Rose and me were still there together with a very strong old woman called Mrs Ndeza. They obviously thought of Mrs Ndeza as an old, uneducated woman, who did not know of or have any need of a bed. But Rose and I refused:

'This is our Mama. We are not going to sleep on a bed and leave her on the floor.'

'Ah, but this old one doesn't know a thing', they argued.

'This is not a question of favours. We have rights to these beds. Don't think that you are favouring Rose and me. This is a matter of rights and we respect our Mama. She will sleep in a bed and one of us will take the floor tonight. But tomorrow we are going to report this.'

They went and got another bed, but we were already preparing for a new battle. The brutal authority of the Boer guards was crumbling, and we sensed that we could get the upper hand if we stood firm. They used to wake us up at 3 o'clock in the morning.

'Rose,' I said, 'they shouldn't wake us that early in the morning, just to make us sit in the cold. That's our next fight.'

'Okay, Vera, I'm with you', Rose said, but we did not want to involve Mrs Ndeza. She was an old woman and not used to dealing with the whites.

'Mrs. Ndeza,' I told her, ' tomorrow we are not going to get up, but you just go out and pretend you are washing your face or something. We'll deal with them. Don't worry.'

Next morning Simama came:

'Get up, up, up, up! Come on, women! Get up!'

We kept our faces under the blankets.

'Where are we going so early in the morning', I asked from under the blanket. Simama was quite surprised. He had not expected this kind of reaction.

'Get up!' he yelled.

'What about you, Rose?' I asked.

'Yah, why are we getting up? Where are we going? It's still dark', Rose answered.

He was definitely shaken, and I think he even feared that we were going to attack him or something. He turned on his heel and ran to the African sergeant.

'What's wrong with them? Are they mad or what? Go wake them up and tell them to sit up and fold their blankets. Go!'

The African sergeant came and talked to us in the vernacular:

'Why are you not waking up?'

'Today, we are finishing this waking up business. It's too early, it's cold and we have nothing to do but fold our blankets and sit on them. It's over, just go back.'

He left and Simama returned:

'You native women!' – he was screaming now – 'You get up! Get up!'

'No, if we are to go somewhere, fine, we'll get up, but otherwise we are not getting up today.'

From that day on we would sleep as long as we liked. We were gaining our rights, little by little.

The First Trial

The inquiry of the Devlin Commission into public resistance to the Federation and the emergency was still going on. A famous British law firm, Dinglefoot and Kellogg, had offered to represent the African detainees for free and came to Nyasaland to do so. They came to interview Rose and me. First they interviewed Rose and the next day it was my turn.

Just before the lawyers arrived in the prison, two officers from the Criminal Investigation Department called me into a small office.

'We have come to charge you with incitement and unlawful assembly', they said.

'Me!'

'Yes, you know very well that you have been inciting the people in Dedza.'

When the Superintendent in Salisbury had asked us to write a statement about our views on what had contributed to the state of emergency, I had given a full account of the incident in Dedza. I had described how the English police had provoked the demonstrators at the courthouse and started to fire on women and schoolchildren. Apparently the CID had read my statement and decided to charge me on the basis of what I had written.

'I want a lawyer', I said.

'You'll have a lawyer. We have our lawyers there in court.'

'Yah, but what lawyers? When Mrs Ntenda and her secretary were tried it took five minutes to get her convicted. I want my own lawyer and I want to see a lawyer now.'

Luckily, Dinglefoot and Kellogg came to interview me the same day. I told them in detail about the provocations and persecutions by the government and the conditions under which we were being detained. They were on their way to Rhodesia to interview other detainees, including Orton, and asked if they could give him a message. I asked them to tell Orton that I had been charged and received summons.

'Summons?' they asked, and I told them of my visitors.

They discussed the matter among themselves. 'We must defend her', they decided, and asked if I knew the names of the two African CID officers who had visited me, but I didn't.

'We'll find out from the police. You'll hear from us', they said.

The CID officers had informed me that my case was set within two or three days, but they never came back to collect me. I am sure it must have scared them that Dinglefoot and Kellogg inquired about my case, but after their rounds of interviews in Nyasaland and Rhodesia, the two British lawyers left and my case was taken up again.

However, Dinglefoot and Kellogg had given Orton my message and he had immediately sent a telegram to his partner at Chirwa and Company, Mr Sakarani. Sakarani was a good friend and very sympathetic to our cause. By the time they wanted to take me to court, he had already visited me, taken statements and prepared to call witnesses. We decided to call Orton and the chairman and secretary of the NAC branch in Dedza as my witnesses. The government could not refuse the calling of witnesses and had to bring Orton from Rhodesia to give evidence in my case.

When the court date came they brought Orton to Zomba Prison. We were waiting in the courtyard and there were a lot of cars around. I saw him sitting in a police Land Rover and went straight there. I got in and we hugged each other before the officers could intervene.

'No, not that. Get out!' Simama hurried over to separate us and put me in another car.

I had hoped that we would get the chance to meet during the court session, but they kept us apart, and I did not see him again.

The testimony of Orton and the NAC officials would obviously have supported my case, but they never even got the opportunity to give evidence. Sakarani's cross-examination of the government's witness, the white commander of the mobile police force unit that had been in Dedza that afternoon, hit the nail on the head and demolished the crown's case almost before it could be made.

'Do you know Chinyanja?' Sakarani asked the police officer. 'Can you speak or do you understand Chinyanja, sir?'

'What's the point here?' the officer asked uneasily. 'Mrs Chirwa speaks English.'

'Yes, we know that very well, but I'm asking you: What language was she speaking that day? Because you must tell the Court what she was saying and how she was inciting these people to riot. What did you hear? Did you understand it?'

'Well, whatever language she was using, she was obviously inciting the crowd.'

'Ah, I see – "whatever language she was using". Mrs Chirwa was speaking to you in English.'

'That's correct.'

'And you understood, but what about the language she was using with the people you are claiming she was inciting. Did you understand a word of that, if I may ask?'

There was silence, and Sakarani continued:

'And what was she wearing?'

I remembered clearly the dress I wore, because Orton had commented on my dress that day.

'I'm asking you, what she was wearing. . . . Did you actually see what Mrs Chirwa was doing that day?'

'Oh, I think she was wearing some sort of blue dress', he finally answered, meekly.

'You think! Let me put it to you that she was not wearing a blue dress, but a yellow dress', Sakarani said.

And the case was finished. Sakarani turned to the Magistrate and submitted that there was no case to answer. The Magistrate ruled that the prosecution had failed to prove anything, and I was acquitted.

I was taken back to Zomba, but I was not released. They kept me in detention for more than a month, until our friends in Britain managed to raise my case in the House of Commons. The brother of a dear friend of ours, Margaret Benoit, knew a Labour MP, who put the question to the House:

'Mrs Vera Chirwa has been acquitted only to be put back in prison. Why is the government keeping innocent people in prison?'

The Nyasaland government gave in to the pressure and sent an information officer, Ms Smith, to see me in prison. She tried to persuade me to take a job in the government, live a quiet life and leave Orton and politics behind.

'I was arrested together with my husband and we are going to be released together, and I have vowed never to take a job in the Nyasaland government again because of the way I was mistreated.'

'Vera, you should be more forgiving', she told me.

'No, I'm not forgiving. Are you forgiving?' I asked her.

'Oh, I've just been sent here to talk to you.'

'Well, you can tell your superiors that I want to be released together with my husband.'

Off she went and after a month's time Sakarani came to visit me:

'Vera, I have a gift for you.'

'What gift?'

'Come', he smiled, and took me outside to his car. Orton was sitting there in the back and I was so happy to see him. Ironically, he was never tried. Instead of targeting the constituent leader of the NAC they charged the housewife, but I think they thought of me as an extremist. Orton was a lawyer and he was always very composed, immaculate and to the book. I was more of an activist and did not hold back. Everything inside me came out. During our detention I was often told that I was 'spoiling' the others, and the prison officers were always complaining and regretting that 'this girl' had been sent to pester them in their prison. Maybe I looked like a girl, but I was a 27-year-old mother of three, and I spoke my mind. I think that must have shaken them a bit: an African woman who could understand things, talk sense and find words and reasons for the resentment she felt when confronted by injustice.

We went straight to see the children. Finally, we were free and united after six months of detention, but my friends, Rose and old Mrs Ndeza were still in prison. I went to see them and we dropped tears.

'It's okay, Vera', Rose said.

'Now, look,' I said, 'I'm going to form an organisation to make sure that the pressure for your release is kept up.'

'That's good. Don't forget us.'

'How can I forget you, when we suffered together?' I asked, and went out to form the League of Malawi Women.

3 *Independence*

We had to pick up our life again after prison. They had emptied Orton's offices, closed down our house and removed all our belongings, but Reverend Doig, who had visited us in prison, offered to have us in the Blantyre Mission Station till we found a house. Reverend Doig told us about a young Tongan man, who had been deported from Rhodesia because of his vocal political activities against the Federation. He was quite lost in Nyasaland, but the missionaries were taking care of him. Orton was also a Tonga by tribe and excited to hear about this young activist, whose name was Aleke Banda. The missionaries brought him to meet us and Orton was impressed:

'That's the kind of young person this country needs. He is fighting for our freedom as well as his own', Orton said, and when we moved into our new house Aleke came to live with us. We adopted him as our son.

The state of emergency had not been lifted and the NAC was still banned. If you used the rallying cry of NAC, 'Kwacha' – which means 'dawn' and symbolised the new beginning we were fighting for – you were arrested and deported on the spot. People were seeking Orton's advice:

'We can't just stop fighting because of this emergency. You're a lawyer. You know the laws. Is there a way around this?'

'There is no way they'll allow the NAC to function again, but we can form another party', Orton suggested, and that's how the old NAC leaders, who were not detained, met and formed the

Malawi Congress Party (MCP) in September 1959.

Orton was elected president. The regionalism and tribalism, which Banda later institutionalised and exploited so fiendishly that it destroys Malawian politics even today, did not matter then. We regarded ourselves as one people united towards a common goal. It was not important whether you were a Northerner or came from the South. Orton could lead the people and that was what counted, but it was not obvious who should be the secretary general.

'Now, I have got an idea', Orton said. 'I have been very impressed by this young man, who stays with me. He is young, but I suggest that we try him out. I will coach him, and if he doesn't perform well we can always look for another one.'

Aleke Banda was only 20 years old, but extraordinarily clever and dedicated, and at the next executive committee meeting he was confirmed as secretary general of the MCP.

The MCP was formed to fight on three fronts: to get the political prisoners out of detention, to abolish the Federation and to fight for our independence. The campaigning took off and we were moving up and down the country to inform the people about the birth of the new party.

'If we don't make noise out here our fellow Malawians will rot in prison – including Dr Banda. It's our duty to fight for their release,' Orton thundered at the MCP meetings and people rallied round him.

Chipembere and the Chisiza brothers were still detained, but when they heard that Orton had formed a new party, they opposed it. Chipembere wrote a long letter from prison stressing that Banda was our leader and warning people not to join Orton. Chiume, who was in London, was also writing letters to the same effect. Unfortunately, the rivalry and suspicion within the top figures of the independence movement constantly raised its ugly head. The young radicals – Chipembere, Chiume and the Chisiza brothers – had a grudge against Orton because of his support back in 1953 for a former NAC leader, Matinga, who had taken a softer stand in opposition to the Federation. They now claimed that Orton's motives could not be trusted and that MCP might be secretly supported by the British to rival Banda and divide and weaken the struggle.

Orton always sought to engage in a dialogue with his adversaries, but he was a very principled man, a law onto himself, who did not fit into political intrigues. During one of his many trips to England at that time, Orton had been approached by the Secretary of State, who offered to make him Prime Minister if he would oppose Dr Banda. The British knew that Orton was more sensible and capable than many of the younger radicals, but he could not be bought and he insisted that all prisoners, including his leader, should be released.

In April 1960, Orton was called to the Governor's house.

'Chirwa, guess what gift we're going to give you today', the Governor said.

'Well, I can't guess', Orton answered, quite puzzled.

Dr Banda was brought in from a room next door, and they hugged, happy to see each other. The Governor had lifted the state of emergency.

'He's free. You can take him', the Governor said, and Orton drove the leader to our house. Orton immediately handed him the presidency of the MCP on a silver platter. In six months, Orton, Aleke and the rest of us had built the broad-based, powerful and well-functioning party that carried Malawi to independence.

The League of Malawi Women

I had been a founding member of the NAC Women's League together with my aunt, Rose Chiwambo, and Mrs Ntenda in the mid-1950s when Manoah Chirwa was president of the NAC. When Banda took over the NAC presidency in 1958, he was given absolute power to appoint NAC executives and he had ordered Rose to re-organize the Women's League of the NAC.

When we formed MCP, Rose and Mrs Ntenda were still in prison and it was obvious that we should form a women's wing of the new party that could press for their release. I convened a meeting and we formed the League of Malawi Women. They wanted to elect me as president, but I refused.

'How can I be president of the MCP women's organisation, when my husband is MCP president? It's not right. It will look like a household affair.'

'But you have the ideas and the vision', they insisted.

'No, we are going to share this vision. Let us elect another one.'

Orton was far ahead of his time on the gender issue and he had made sure that two women, Mrs Malanga and Mrs Khonje, were already part of the MCP executive. We elected Mrs Malanga as the first president of the League of Malawi Women, and I accepted the post as organising secretary, because I felt very strongly about organising the women in the villages. We formulated the same objectives as the MCP: to fight for our freedom, for the abolition of the Federation and for the release of all the political prisoners, but we added the emphasis on teaching our fellow women about their rights.

The state of emergency was still on and there was curfew. People were afraid and it was difficult to organise them. I started in Zomba, where my sister was living. We did not have a car and had to walk from home to home for more than two weeks.

'Oh, we are going to get shot,' most of them said. They were very afraid.

'Now, look, if we just keep quiet, Chipembere, Rose Chiwambo and the others will not come out.' I had heard Orton talk like that, when he was addressing the people. 'We must fight! We must organise ourselves. It's the only way to freedom.'

I managed to enrol 15 women and we formed the first local branch of the League of Malawi Women. From there we moved to the next district. The MCP executive committee gave us a Volkswagen and by the time the emergency was lifted, we had organised branches all over the country.

It was hard work. Orton was building up MCP branches here and I was busy organising the women there. We seldom met in the house and only for a short time. Our children were growing up without their parents and they missed us, but we had to let them suffer for the moment:

'When we get self-government', Orton and I told each other, 'it will be alright again.'

To make it even more demanding, I was expecting our fourth child.

My colleagues did not understand how I could work so tirelessly and be so pregnant. In fact, the baby was almost born during a campaign meeting. We were in Chikwawa, which is a very hot place full of mosquitoes, and I felt bad. I was somehow constipated and had to use the toilet of a woman we visited. The woman was a relative of mine, and when I did not come back she started to worry.

'Mama, are you alright in there?' she asked.

'No!' I was totally paralysed and could not move.

She hauled me out of there: 'Maybe you are going to deliver.'

'No, I'm just constipated', I said, but she called a taxi and sent me off to Queen Elizabeth Hospital.

It was a beautiful hospital, but it was segregated. In principle, it was just a matter of paying a fee, but the few African patients who might have been able to pay did not know that. The staff never encouraged Africans to choose the well-equipped paying section of the hospital, or even offered them that choice – and so, in practice, the whites had that section for themselves.

Orton had a good income from his law firm and we often hosted parties with both African and white guests. I remember discussing my pregnancy at one of these parties with the superintendent of the 'European' section of Queen Elizabeth Hospital and Lady Glyn Jones, the Governor's wife.

'Don't you attend antenatal clinic, Vera?' they wanted to know.

'No, I don't. The treatment in the African section is bad and faulty. I went there once and that was more than enough for me.'

'But it's important for you. You should come to my section. It's of course a matter of paying, but I'm sure you can afford it', the superintendent said.

'Ah, since when is it only a matter of paying?' I was quite surprised. 'Why don't you tell people that?'

From that day, I attended antenatal clinic in the paying section, and what a drama. All the pregnant white women were sitting in line waiting for the doctor, but they would not sit next to me. When I sat down beside them, they simply got up from their chairs and moved away. It was fine with me because it allowed me to move up the line. They really feared my black skin, but they got used to it and eventually we started talking.

By the time I was brought to the hospital from Chikwawa they had accepted me and I went straight in. The sisters treated my constipation, but they thought labour was about to start and wanted to admit me. I did not have time and went back on the road. Two days later we were somewhere near Ndora, when I really felt the labour pains. Luckily Orton was around and took me back to the hospital, where a baby boy was born.

We were in the middle of a fight for our freedom and Orton

named our son 'Nkhondo', which means war in our language. A few days after Nkhondo was born there was a large MCP meeting and Orton went to tell Dr Banda that we had been blessed with a baby boy.

'Mr Chirwa,' the leader said, 'I want to bless this child. Can I give him my own name?'

'Yes, you can', Orton said, and at the meeting Dr Banda proudly addressed the MCP delegates from all over the country:

'We are missing one of our women leaders, Mrs Vera Chirwa, here today. Well, I'm happy to tell you that Mr and Mrs Chirwa have received a precious gift, a strong and healthy boy, and I name him Kamuzu!'

There was a roar and a great applause and our baby boy became very famous. Women came to dance for him and we received many lambs, goats and gifts for our little Nkhondo Kamuzu Chirwa.

The Amazon Army

We had the first democratic elections in 1961. MCP won a landslide victory and Dr Banda became Minister of Natural Resources and Local Government. Governor Glyn Jones, who had replaced Governor Armitage, was assigned to direct the country towards independence in collaboration with the MCP. He thought highly of Dr Banda, who quickly became *de facto* chief minister. However, about 12 of our fellow freedom fighters were still detained, including Chipembere and the Chisiza brothers. It was not clear why the leader did not push for their release. It was no secret that he considered the young radicals to be extremists. He might have been afraid that their strong pan-African and anti-colonial views would spoil the negotiations with the British. He was also busy regaining control of MCP, and he probably wanted to minimise any challenge to his authority.

Orton was their friend and lawyer and he often visited them in Kangedza Prison near Blantyre.

'Orton, we depend on you. Please talk to Banda. We're tired of imprisonment.' They were becoming desperate and Orton went to see the leader, only to come back more frustrated:

'I don't know what's wrong with Kamuzu Banda! He has the power to tell the Governor to release these people, but he doesn't want to.'

I decided to organise the League of Malawi Women around this issue and called the executive committee together for a meeting.

'We should campaign to get these people free. I think we should start to harass the guards. Let's make a camp outside the prison and swamp them with women visitors.'

From that day, groups of women from the different branches of the League of Malawi Women took turns to camp outside the prison. It really annoyed the prison authorities, but what could they do?

The prisoners realised that we were seriously fighting for them and they poured their troubles out to us when we were allowed to bring them some food. I managed to talk with Chipembere.

'Vera, we know Orton is doing his best and that Banda is unwilling. We are feeling that he doesn't want us to come out.'

'We don't want to see you suffer in here any longer', I assured him.

'Then please do something. You women are our only hope', Chipembere said.

We left the prison. The sun was setting and our group went into the forest and sat down.

'Now, people, let us sit here and decide what we can do for them. They are suffering and they are depending on us now.'

We started to discuss and I suggested that we should stage a strike.

'What kind of strike?' they asked.

'I've read of different kinds of strikes. We can do a sit-down strike or we can do a demonstration with placards and what not', I said.

We settled on a sit-down strike.

'Now you should know that it can be tough. The police might teargas us or even kill us. Some of us have been through these things before', I cautioned them.

'No, we are not going to surrender. We are not afraid!' they shouted.

'Are you sure?' I asked again.

'Yes! Our men are suffering and we have to help them.'

We decided to divide ourselves in groups but act in concert, with simultaneous sit-down strikes at Government House, the Secretary's house, the provincial headquarters and so on, but we also agreed that I should take Orton's advice on this before we launched our campaign. I went home and chatted with Orton over dinner:

'We managed to meet the detainees today. They are really suffering.'

'Yes, it's bad. Kamuzu is terrible. As his legal adviser I'm telling him he has the power to release them. Maybe he fears them. I don't know the real reason,' Orton said.

I told him about our plan to launch a series of sit-down strikes. Orton thought it was excellent and a bit dangerous, but it was not the British guns that he was most worried about.

'Vera, I must tell you that Kamuzu is going to be nasty. Will you stand up to him?'

'Yes I will. The women are my strength. We have all agreed on this. We are serious and we are going to do it.'

'Okay, but let me give you some good advice about your approach to Kamuzu – don't be aggressive. Tell him softly that we all know the prisoners are suffering and since you women are certain that he is working hard to get them free you are approaching him to offer a helping hand.'

We were quite close to the leader. Orton was not only the legal adviser of the NAC but also its president's personal lawyer, while Dr Banda was our family doctor. We even went to him at night, when the children were sick, and he took care of them.

'Don't trust the white doctors, Mrs Chirwa,' he said, 'these times are too political. Just bring the children to me.'

Orton knew Dr Banda better than most other people and he coached us very well.

We made an appointment with him for the following day at 4 o'clock – the whole executive of the League of Malawi Women, including some of our branch leaders.

'My Amazon Army!' the leader said when he came to greet us. 'Have a seat. What is the problem? Have you just come to see me?'

I was the spokesperson and told him of our plan exactly as Orton had suggested. But I saw his face changing.

'Now, Mrs Chirwa, do you know what you are getting into? Do you know where you are leading these women?'

'Yes, we know.'

'No, listen, are you sure? They are going to be shot at by the police. They will be arrested and put in prison – including you, of course.'

'But the women are very determined. I explained to them that they could be shot, teargassed and imprisoned, but they want these people to be set free.'

'Have you considered this carefully, because I don't think it's a good idea. No, it's not good.'

'Sir, these people have been suffering in prison for almost two years. They have families. They have work to do. Should they just rot there? They are our children and we women really feel for them. That's why we decided to go and speak with our *Ngwazi*.*

Ngwazi: a title that Dr Banda took for himself meaning 'great warrior', making his full title Ngwazi Dr Hastings Kamuzu Banda, Life President of Malawi.

You have too much on your hands and we want to help you.'

We had decided to give Dr Banda a little time to organise the release before we launched the campaign, and the upcoming MCP convention in Nkhotakota was only three weeks away.

'Please tell the Governor that your women want these people released before the convention in Nkhotakota, and if he refuses you can tell him that we are prepared to do a sit-down strike', I concluded.

'A sit-down strike? Do you know how dangerous that is? They are going to beat you up!'

He kept quiet for some time, looking at us very seriously. I thought he was going to jump up and throw us out, but we kept calm and just looked back at him.

'Okay, I must think about it', he finally said. We left and laughed and giggled outside in reaction to the tense situation we had managed with a fair amount of success.

A week later we were called to his residence.

'The prisoners are going to be released', he told us and we were very happy. 'My women are very strong. My Amazon Army – I like that.'

I went home and told Orton, who was also pleased: 'You women! It's very good that women stand up for things. Let's hope he is going to actually do it.'

The convention in Nkhotakota was opened. Orton, who was now vice-president, Aleke, who was still secretary general, the Youth League and the League of Malawi Women had organised everything. MCP had collected a lot of money from members and well-wishers, but there was some confusion over the party funds and the party delegates were eager to hear the financial report at the convention. We had lost NAC's money because of the emergency and the leader had apparently transferred the MCP funds out of the country to safeguard them if the party was banned.

However, the financial report was continuously being delayed. In fact, there were a lot of *ad hoc* meetings, backstage gossip and informal high-level talks. These intrigues confused and frustrated everybody, except Dr Banda, who was the master of them all.

To our surprise, during the leader's speech the 12 prisoners came on stage. They had been sent straight from the prison to the convention, where Dr Banda had met them on his own. He manipulated them against Orton and convinced them that he should become 'life president' of the MCP.

'I have talked to the Governor', he announced from the stage, 'You are now free.'

He had secretly made Mrs Ntenda of our Zomba branch manufacture 12 reddish robes and caps to honour them for what they had achieved.

'Mrs Ntenda', he called, 'come and robe our "prison graduates"!'

The delegates, of course, were jubilant. The leader never mentioned our effort. Obviously, mentioning my name would have boosted Orton, whose popularity Dr Banda wanted to undermine, but we did not care about the acknowledgement as long as the prisoners were out and free.

Suddenly, Dunduzu Chisiza got up, a move which really infuriated Orton.

'All of us are equal here. We need an elder to lead us, to whom nobody can be second.' Here Chisiza was directing his speech at Orton, who was still vice-president. 'Kamuzu Banda is one of his own and below him we all become equal. Now, since we have such a person as Kamuzu Banda, and since we all love him so much, don't we all want him to be life president?'

People were confused. They had put youth leaders on the front rows, who were shouting and dancing and deliberately making it hard to understand what was actually going on. Pamphlets with a picture of the leader as 'life president' were quickly distributed and the new title was confirmed. Orton had been couped again and he was shocked.

'This is quite uncalled for', he complained to me. 'My col-leagues have always been jealous of me, but to write the vice-presidency of the party off like that! I have done a lot to organise the people, and that's why they are out of prison.'

'It doesn't matter', I comforted him.

'No, Vera, it does matter. This is how dictators are made!'

Dancing with the Duke

Orton was disregarded at the convention, but people on the street thought very highly of him and he was still strongly associated with the party he had built up. Such well-established public support was a thorn in Banda's flesh and over the following period a lot of the MCP leaders close to Orton were replaced. The executive of the League of Malawi Women was also changed and Rose Chiwambo became our new chairperson after she was let out of prison. Kamuzu was a master at playing people off against each other and bickering even started among the women leaders. It annoyed some of them that they received less applause and public recognition than me, formally a mere organising secretary. They complained to the leader, who started to castigate me and accuse me of having personal ambitions, but I let it all pass. I did not have time for intrigues. I was fully occupied as a housewife, activist and now also a student.

'I think you had better start studying again, Vera', Orton had said. 'I want to fulfil my promise to your parents. It's also best in case something happens to me and you have to take care of the family.'

I started to take my A levels through a South African corres-pondence course, but I was also expecting our fifth child. I was very big and we were both very excited, because we wanted to have twins. However, it was just one big baby and he was reluctant to come out. I was well into the tenth month and Orton kept postponing an official visit to London.

'Now, look, Orton, you just go', I told him.

'No, I don't want to leave you like this. I'll wait till the baby comes', he insisted.

'You go! It's you who is stopping this baby from coming out', I joked, and off he went.

I was finishing the correspondence course and had to go all the way to Zomba to sit for my exams. I went on a Thursday and sat for English literature and English language the next day. The economics and constitutional law exams were scheduled for Tuesday, but on Saturday the baby came. I gave birth to our youngest son at Queen Elizabeth Hospital. I was taken to a maternity ward with two white women and I immediately started studying.

'What is this dry stuff you are reading, Mrs Chirwa? Put it away and take a women's magazine instead', the doctor insisted, but as soon as he was gone I picked up my books again.

'Mrs Chirwa, these books are too dry for you', the nurses complained. 'You have to rest.'

'But I have an examination to write on Tuesday', I told them.

'No, no, no, you are far too tired.'

I begged the doctor to let me go for the exam.

'But what about the baby', he asked bewildered.

'I have a basket for the baby.'

'And the mosquitoes?'

'I have a net.' Finally he let me go.

Tuesday at 9 o'clock I went to the examination room in Zomba. There were four other candidates, all men. Shortly after we started writing, I heard the baby, who was in the car with a nanny, starting to cry. I felt bad and rose to leave my desk. The examination official came to me.

'What's the problem, Mrs Chirwa?'

'My baby is crying. I have to go and feed my baby.'

He then ran ahead of me to the car.

'Take the baby away', he told the driver, 'It's disturbing the mother. Go away!'

I went back to my desk and started answering the questions. Economics and constitutional law are difficult subjects and it was hard for me to concentrate, but I sat through it and handed in my paper.

I was certain that I had failed. When the results came, I immediately recognised the South African stamp on the envelope and went to the toilet to open my letter in private. I came out dancing. I had passed! I sent a telegram to Orton in London and he enrolled me in the Faculty of Law at the University College of London. He brought back Part One of the Bar Exam and I began to read and read. I passed everything except Roman Law by correspondence and in October 1963 I left for London to finish my Bar Exam.

Orton sent me a ticket to come home and attend the independence celebrations in July 1964. The Queen's husband, The Duke of Edinburgh, came to represent the British government. When we reached State House to celebrate we were all disturbed by the fact that a barrier had been put up with Dr Banda, The Duke, Kadzamira and the other dignitaries on one side and the rest of us on the other. The hall was simply cut in two by a rope and we were surprised and rather displeased to find a barrier at our own independence celebration.

Dr Banda opened the dance with Lady Glyn Jones, the Governor's wife, and the Duke danced with Kadzamira. Cecilia Kadzamira was originally Dr Banda's nurse and secretary, when he opened a small clinic in Blantyre just after he returned in 1958. They were very close and she continued as his personal secretary when he became President. The leader never married and

President Banda opening the dance with the Governor's wife, Lady
Glyn Jones, at the independence celebrations, 6 July 1964

Courtesy of The Society of Malawi

Kadzamira also acted as the nation's first lady at functions like this.

On our side of the barrier we were all dancing and celebrating
– except Orton. Our friends were teasing us:

'Are you not going to dance?'

'Come now, my husband. Everybody's enjoying it here, dance
with me!' but he was too shy and asked one of his friends to take
his place on the dance floor.

Dr Banda never stayed long at parties. Even with a chief guest

as important as the Duke of Edinburgh, he left early. Although Dr
Banda was afraid of Orton and tried to hold him down, he was
also very fond of my husband. I think he respected Orton's
education and class and somehow regarded him as more dignified
and responsible than the rest of the ministers. He referred to his
minister as 'my boys', which they of course felt very offended by,
except Orton, whom he always called 'Mr Chirwa'. That evening
the leader sent for Orton:

'Mr Chirwa, I'm leaving now. Look after our guest, the Duke
of Edinburgh.'

Orton and I then crossed the barrier and I danced with the
Duke. It was a special moment to dance with this ultimate repre-
sentative of the British Empire in celebration of the freedom for
which we had fought so hard. After Dr Banda had left the Duke
broke the barrier down. He removed the rope and went to dance
with almost every woman at the party. People were very pleased.

'Yah, why should we be discriminated against at our own
celebration?' people said and everybody applauded the Duke for
opening the dance floor.

The following day in Parliament the Duke was to hand over the
government formally to Dr Banda, President of our new nation,
Malawi. It was a great moment. However, Chiume, who was in
charge of celebrations, had found that there was no room for the
women and wives of the ministers in the chamber itself. We were
to sit in another room and hear the ceremony on some
loudspeakers. Orton had heard about this arrangement from
Chiume and told me on the way to the ceremony.

'No, I don't think that's right! The women of Malawi have
fought so hard. When you men were fighting on your own, you
had no impact. When the women joined the fight we really got
somewhere, and now that we have our freedom you want to close
us up in a room? To do what? We don't want to hear the ceremony.
We want to see it.'

'I don't know, Mama. They say there are too many invitees', Orton said. 'I'm just warning you that you might not be able to enter the chamber for the ceremony.'

When we reached Parliament the police stopped me.

'I want to pass', I insisted.

'No, you go over there', they said and sent me away.

In the room I found Mrs Chipembere, Mrs Bwanausi, Rose's husband, Edwin, and a few others.

'Did you agree to just sit in this room?' I asked them.

'No,' they said, 'but we were forced to come here.'

'We can't stay here. We have fought for this day. We have to go inside.'

'Yah, Vera, come on and fight for us', they urged me smilingly.

I went straight to the police guards, who tried to stop me, but I pressed past them:

'Leave me alone! I have something to do inside here.'

There were plenty of seats inside. Chipembere, who loved me very much, saw me and called me over:

'Vera, come here and sit. Why are our women left outside?'

Yatuta Chisiza also joined in: 'Yah, come on Vera – fight, fight!'

They all laughed and encouraged me, except Chiume, who had made the arrangement, and whose wife, of course, was not there.

'Yah, I'm fighting. We are coming in. Who are all these white women that have been invited? Did they fight to experience this day?'

I went to collect the others. We ended up filling the whole section where Kadzamira and the white women dignitaries should have sat, and they had to move over on the MPs side. Everybody congratulated me, and at the garden party afterwards, Kadzamira approached me:

'What is all this now? Why is everybody congratulating you like a little hero?' she asked.

'I fought for the Malawi women to enter the chamber', I said,

'We were supposed to have been sitting in a room next door.'

Kadzamira was not happy about that and it only made things worse that I took her place later in the evening when the Duke insisted on having me as his dinner partner.

In spite of the personal intrigues and petty jealousy it was hard not to be overwhelmed by joy and excitement. We had won our independence and it was a time full of hope and euphoria. Thus, we had named our youngest son Zengani, which means 'peace' or 'build something up'. But Banda was soon to destroy all that.

The tension between Malawi's leader and his senior ministers had been building up over the years leading up to independence, but Orton and his colleagues had nevertheless united behind Dr Banda. They had given him the undisputed leadership of the freedom movement in order to stand as firm and focused as possible against the colonisers. No matter how clearly the leader's dictatorial tendencies revealed themselves, or how far his policies departed from the ministers' ideas for our new nation, no conflicts within the movement were allowed to delay independence. But after independence matters came to the boil – and the lid came off when Dr Banda returned from the OAU meeting in Cairo soon after independence.

When he returned from abroad the ministers and their wives always had to go to his house and welcome him. That particular day chairs were put up on his veranda as usual, but there were only chairs for the ministers, not for the wives. We were a bit confused, but then Bwanausi, who was Minister of Social Development, got up and gave his chair to his wife. The other ministers followed suit and all of them had to stand. It was simply a cheap trick to humiliate them and make them stand like school children before a headmaster when Dr Banda came in.

He immediately started to denounce Chipembere and Chiume. He was very angry and even tried to turn us women against our own husbands.

'You, my women', he said. 'Watch them! Some of my trusted

cabinet ministers are conspiring with foreign powers. You watch them!'

Chiume was Foreign Minister and had obviously been in his element among the many pan-Africanist statesmen at the OAU meeting. Dr Banda no doubt felt upstaged and he reacted very harshly. Foreign policy was a matter of great dispute between the leader and the ministers, who were strongly opposed to his cooperation with apartheid South Africa and the Portuguese colonial powers in neighbouring Mozambique. Dr Banda, for his part, accused the pan-Africanist young radicals of mounting a communist conspiracy – especially Chiume, who had been instrumental in organising a substantial offer of aid from China, which the President refused to accept.

Dr Banda's accusations of conspiracy and his humiliation of the ministers that evening urged them to confront him, and they met in secret to decide what to do. The leader was openly attacking their authority and he had recently dismissed John Msonthi from his post as Minister of Transport. Msonthi was later reinstated, but his dismissal made it clear to the ministers that the President was capricious and would sacrifice those close to him without batting an eyelid.

Msonthi's dismissal was a telling sign of Dr Banda's personal weaknesses. He wanted absolute control over the system of power, including Parliament, and in the general elections he had ordered the ministers and other MCP leaders to stifle any opposition to his own handpicked candidates.

'Elections are coming', the leader had said, 'and I'm going to choose the candidates myself for every constituency. If somebody opposes my candidate, you deal with him. You know what I mean. I want no opposition!'

Obviously, there were opposing candidates, and I heard from London, where I was by then studying law, that violence had broken out in some constituencies. In Orton's constituency the old NAC strongman, T. D. T. Banda, opposed him, but Orton won without the violence that many of the others did not scruple to use. In the constituencies where opposing candidates were intimidated people did not complain and Dr Banda got away with it. Except in one case.

A prominent MCP candidate had stood for election in Nkhotakota. The opposing candidate, who had challenged him, had been killed and he had ended up standing unopposed, according to Dr Banda's orders. However, the people of Nkhotakota are very proud – just like the Tonga of Nkhata Bay. They sent a delegation straight to the leader and complained:

'What is all this? We set up a candidate ourselves and he was killed. He was murdered and this MCP candidate had a hand in it.'

Dr Banda was our family doctor and he stayed with us a number of times. Orton and I were close to him and knew his strengths and weaknesses. He was a very strong dictator, but he also wanted credit. He craved recognition and was quick to take credit for the successes of his subordinates. He was just as quick to wash his hands of a failure.

'What?' he said to the Nkhotakota delegates. 'I don't want any violence. I'll deal with it.'

The candidate, who had followed orders, was dismissed.

But the ministers were reacting to more than Dr Banda's style of leadership. In addition to foreign policy, they disagreed fundamentally with Dr Banda's political course on a number of points. First of all, the ministers disagreed with Dr Banda's acceptance of the recommendations of the Skinner Commission, which was set up prior to independence to look into the conditions of the civil service. Dr Banda was unwilling to Africanise the civil service and replace the white civil servants after independence as many of the ministers wanted. Following the recommendations of the Skinner Report, it was decided that the salaries of white civil servants would be raised, whereas the salaries of African civil servants would remain static. The African civil servants were in uproar:

'Why are we to be paid less? We go to the same market. We go to the same shops. The whites are already getting a lot of money and now the gap is supposed to be even greater!'

Another contentious issue was the recent introduction of a three-penny charge at government hospitals. My return from London for the independence celebrations coincided with the annual nation-wide tour of the League of Malawi women and Rose Chiwambo had asked me to come along. During that tour we received a lot of complaints from the village women:

'We women have been used to giving birth at home in our villages. Then you encourage us to go to the hospital – and when we respond you decide to charge a fee!'

Three pennies was a modest fee, but it could mean all the difference to poor people, and the staff at the hospitals were taking advantage of the situation by exaggerating the fee or rejecting people who were unable to pay. After the tour we presented a list to Dr Banda of stories collected from the villages about penniless women who had been left to give birth on the roadside or been sent back from hospital in a critical situation.

People were quite upset and the ministers and the MPs sensed a general public dissatisfaction. Dr Banda had launched a self-help scheme and encouraged people to participate in building the new Malawi:

'If you want to develop the country don't leave it to the government alone. We must all work very hard because Malawi is poor. You build schools and the government will provide the teachers. You build hospitals and houses for the staff and the government will provide the doctors. You grow cabbages and tomatoes and make a road to the market, and if you need a bridge the government will build it for you.'

The League of Malawi Women, the Youth League, the ministers and the MPs had campaigned tirelessly, and the response was formidable. People built things, but where were the doctors, the teachers and the bridges? They felt that the government had failed to deliver its part of the deal; people complained that the tomatoes and cabbage were rotting in the gardens.

Many MPs approached the ministers with these complaints:

'We are getting unpopular in our own constituencies. You have to approach Dr Banda.'

The ministers decided to take all these complaints to the leader, but nobody had ever challenged his authority. He had a temper and flared up very violently; everybody, including the ministers, was afraid of him. They knew it was a critical moment for them all and decided to stand together.

'What happened to Msonthi should not be repeated', Orton said. 'If one person is sacked we should stand together.'

Orton, who was Minister of Justice, and Chipembere, who was Minister of Education, had both made arrangements to go abroad. Chipembere was going to a conference in Canada and Orton was on his way to Britain. Orton decided to cancel his trip, but Chipembere had to leave:

'I must go, but anything you decide – good or bad – I'm with you. We have made a promise to each other. Kamuzu's tactics are to divide and rule and if he expels even one of us, we'll all resign.'

At a Cabinet meeting in August 1964 the ministers presented their grievances.

'Where did you find the courage!' Dr Banda exclaimed, and started singling people out:

'You, Chiume! Since when did you become my adviser?'

The President was so shocked by the criticism that he offered to resign.

'I'm resigning and going back to my home in Britain', he said, but they rejected his resignation and, by the conclusion of the meeting, he had calmed down and seemed to have taken note of their complaints about his policies.

'I'm going to think about it', he said.

The ministers had the impression that the meeting had ended amicably and that discussion on the disputed policies would now continue. In the meantime Dr Banda called in other key officials like the Speaker, the provincial governors and senior MPs, and questioned them about the situation.

'Is it true that the people are against my government?' he wanted to know, and I think he was being misled.

'No, *Ngwazi*, the ministers are conspiring against you. They just want to take over', they told him, and deliberately made mischief between the leader and his ministers to take advantage of the situation. Dr Banda then started to make new alliances and promised people seats in the government in return for their support. He sent the Speaker to win over Rose Chiwambo, but Rose was very close to Orton and Chipembere and she had listened to people's complaints during our tour with the League of Malawi Women.

'No, when people like Chirwa, Chisiza and Chipembere are pointing out these problems that I've seen with my own eyes, I'm with them. People are being oppressed here!' Rose said.

'Oh no, Rose, let's support Kamuzu Banda. Remember he is the one who appointed you.'

'No, I'm not supporting Banda. I'm a woman of principle.'

Rose did not even receive a proper letter of dismissal. She realised that she had been sacked at the next parliamentary session, but things had hotted up a lot more by then.

Governor Glyn Jones and the British were generally behind Dr Banda, but the Governor called the ministers in and encouraged them to name a leader who could take over if the President resigned.

'Give me a name, so I can announce a new leader', he said.

The ministers agreed on Orton as their candidate.

'They are saying that I should take over', he came home to tell me, 'and I have accepted, but who is going to announce it? I can't announce it myself. It's embarrassing. I think the others are going to put forward my name to Glyn Jones.'

But nothing happened. The country was in a limbo and Glyn Jones was getting impatient. He asked the ministers to present their case in writing, in order for him to mediate between them and Dr Banda. Chiume wrote the letter.

Unfortunately, the letter was a great mistake. Chiume included personal attacks that had nothing to do with the political substance of the conflict and greatly upset both the Governor and Banda. The rift widened even more and on Monday 7 September, the President recalled Parliament for an emergency sitting the following day at which he dismissed Orton, Bwanausi, Chiume and Rose Chiwambo from their posts under accusations of conspiracy. Yatuta Chisiza, who was Minister of Home Affairs, and Chokani, who was Labour Minister, resigned in sympathy the same day.

The Famous Parliament Session

It was war. I had not fully grasped the gravity of the situation and, expecting a normal parliamentary session, innocently went there to sit with the other ministers' wives as usual. Dr Banda started to speak and attacked ruthlessly:

'These ministers want to take my position. They are plotting to kill me', he claimed.

It was chaotic. They had put loudspeakers outside Parliament and brought in die-hard Banda supporters, who roared and protested.

He really denounced the ministers and managed to turn the House and the people outside against them. Kadzamira was yelling at Orton and even Aleke Banda's wife turned against Orton and me. As we walked shakily out of the Parliament building to the screaming crowd outside, Orton and I were holding hands as usual.

'There they go, hand in hand', Aleke's wife sang out mockingly.

We had hosted her and Aleke's marriage in our house and they were as good as our own children. Aleke used to call Orton 'father'. It was devastating. In fact, Aleke was accused of secretly reporting to Dr Banda during those fatal days and betraying Orton and the others. The ministers had held a crucial meeting in Chipembere's house in Mangochi and had not invited Aleke. He was secretary general of MCP and not a member of the Cabinet, but he was part of the inner circle and it had wounded Aleke greatly that he had been left out. Perhaps the leader came up with an attractive offer. In any case, Aleke decided to follow Dr Banda.

That first day of the 'Famous Parliament Session', as it was called, was more than enough for me and I decided not to go the following day, when the ministers made their reply.

Chipembere had rushed back from Canada and gave a brilliant speech on the second day.

'It is not true that we want to topple Dr Banda. We just want to put things right. We are in touch with the people and are the ones who hear their complaints. There are complaints from all sides and we want to talk about these problems and put them right.'

Chipembere told the House that the President had tried to win him to his side the minute he landed at Chileka Airport, but Chipembere was a man of honour and stood by his word to his colleagues. They all presented their cases well and the mood was turning in their favour. People were applauding them.

But to the surprise of Orton and the others Msonthi, who had been recalled as Transport Minister, did not stand up for his colleagues. They had expected his support and he had taken part in the meeting in Mangochi, but he had in fact run back to the leader and told on the others.

'The ministers are saying that if you dismiss one of them they will all resign. Chirwa is advising them that if they are all dismissed you will have to dissolve Parliament, and they can then go back to their constituencies and stand as independents in the new elections.'

And the leader had tempted him.

'I made you suffer when I dismissed you, Msonthi, but this time I'll look after you.'

It had been hard on Msonthi, that first dismissal. He was under intense pressure and the others forgave his weakness.

The ministers met immediately after the Famous Parliament Session. Although they had defended themselves well against Dr Banda's attack, they knew he wanted them out of the way and they felt very threatened. Dr Banda was obviously about to unleash the dreaded party storm troops, the Young Pioneers, on the ministers and their supporters. Violence was in the air and it was adeptly organised by MCP strongmen still loyal to Dr Banda. The ministers decided to go back and consult their constituencies: we went to Orton's village near Nkatha Bay.

Dr Banda called all the District Commissioners of Malawi to a meeting to make sure he could count on their support. We happened to know the District Commissioner of Nkatha Bay very well; when he came back from the meeting he told us of rumours that the leader was going to confiscate my passport. I would have been unable to finish my studies, but Orton reacted swiftly. We rushed to Zambia, from where I flew back to London.

Orton passed Blantyre on the way back to collect some things from our house. We had packed and left for Nkatha Bay as quickly as possible and had forgotten some of the children's clothes and Orton's suits. When he reached Blantyre, he learned that the others were organising a big public meeting.

'Chirwa', Chipembere said, 'don't go back to Nkatha Bay. Let's

Marathon session of Parliament

Dr. BANDA WINS VOTE OF CONFIDENCE

Chip says why he resigned

Motion goes through without dissent

A VOTE of confidence in the policies of the Prime Minister, Dr. Banda, was carried without dissent on Wednesday evening after a non-stop marathon session of nearly 11 hours, the longest in the history of the Malawi Parliament.

The Prime Minister emphasised in a closing speech to the House that this was not a "crisis," but a "domestic affair that would be solved." He said he bore his ministers no ill will, and he believed them when they declared their loyalty.

Dr. Banda said he was not afraid of this debate, and that it must be finished. He wanted to find out if the people were tired of him, or whether they wanted his ministers instead. Everybody was able to express their views, and he wanted a decision, one way or the other.

Decision on Peking

On Red China, he said that this problem was poisoning international relationships and that 700 million people could not be ignored. This was an international matter and he would work through the United Nations.

He said the Chinese must ask him, saying: "Kamuzu, you must recognise us, we are a great people, an ancient people, we are 700 million in number. When they talk so, I will understand, but not the language of bribery. Not by dangling a nebulous £6 million, before my eyes, not £18 million, or even £100 million."

He said he was not going to give way under duress. He would rather resign first, or be shot like President Olympio of Togo.

He said he would not scrap the Skinner report just like that. He was a Prime Minister with a spine. He had asked the British Government to prepare this report. He was going to Britain in November, and he could hardly face the British Chancellor if he had scrapped a report he had asked them to prepare.

The Prime Minister is holding a Press conference at 9 a.m. on Friday morning in Zomba.

(A report of Dr. Banda's opening speech appears on Page 7)

Mr. Masauko Chipembere took a seat on the back benches at the beginning of Wednesday morning's debate signifying his resignation as Minister of Education.

He said he had resigned because his colleagues had been sacked on insufficient grounds. He said: "I came back from Canada to find the Prime Minister believing anonymous letters."

He went on: "It would be an act of betrayal if I remained in the Government while my friends are branded as traitors." He said the Premier had denounced innocent people in public, listening to only one

Front page of *The Daily Times* at the height of the Cabinet Crisis,
September 1964

Courtesy of *The Daily Times*

address the people and tell them our side of the story so they know what really happened.'

The ministers gathered a big crowd, but then violence broke out. Dr Banda had brought in truckloads of young, rowdy villagers from Port Herald, who had no idea of what was really afoot but had been ordered to sabotage the meeting and beat everybody up. The situation was explosive and the ministers decided to disperse the meeting. They did not like to see innocent Malawians killing each other and they did not want to use force. Chiume, Chokani and Bwanausi fled to Zambia the same evening and Rose, Chipembere, Chisiza and Orton decided to head back to the safety of their home areas.

That evening some high-placed civil servants, who as a group generally supported the ministers, called Chipembere on the phone and warned him.

'Tell the ministers that they must travel tonight. The police are everywhere and they are out to harm you people. You have to get out of here now!'

After the meeting Orton had gone back to finish packing, but Chipembere could not get hold of him, because we had recently moved to a new house. The urgent warning never reached Orton, but thank God he decided to take off that evening anyway.

The Burning Car

When he reached the river crossing at Thondwe, he was stopped by a police patrol. It was at exactly the same place where Dunduzu Chisiza, who had hidden under our bed during the first days of the emergency, died in 1962 in a mysterious car accident that Dr Banda is rumoured to have organised. The police just looked into Orton's car and told the driver to carry on.

A bit further down a huge tree had been felled, which blocked the road completely. The driver started to reverse and suddenly there were people everywhere. They had cut a tree on the Zarewa Road to catch Orton, but his bodyguard, John Chirwa, had changed the route. *This* tree was actually meant to catch Chipembere. Both ministers drove grey Mercedes Benzes, so the group of Young Pioneers, who had been waiting in the darkness, stormed out to take their prey when they saw the car.

'Chipembere!' they screamed. 'You are dying tonight. You will not see another tomorrow!'

But Chipembere had been delayed in Blantyre and Orton was now in serious trouble. All the ministers had distinct licence plates and the Pioneers quickly realised that they had caught another big fish.

'It's Chirwa! It's Chirwa! Let's finish him instead!', they yelled.

Orton's bodyguard had been in South Africa, and I think he had been exposed to a lot of things down there, because he was exceptionally good at his work. He reacted very quickly, ordered the driver to back up the car and hit the brakes, and shouted to Orton:

'Sir, get out of the car on this side. We'll go on the other side!'

It was dark and Orton jumped out unnoticed. John and the driver managed to mislead the Pioneers by running in the opposite direction.

'There he goes! There he goes!' they shouted, and the Pioneers followed them.

Orton quickly hid in a ditch. John and the driver ran as far as they could. Orton never saw them again.

The Pioneers came back towards the car disappointed.

'Where is he? Where is he?'

From his hiding place in the dark, Orton heard their leader cry out in despair:

'Ah, what am I going to tell Banda? I was asked to bring the heads of Chirwa and Chipembere – and where is he now?'

Thank God they did not find him. Instead the Pioneers destroyed the car. They stole all our clothes from the boot, put grass underneath the car, set fire to it, and left. A bit further down the road the police looked on passively. They were just there to take the dead bodies away. Orton started to walk and got lost.

Soon the news broke that Orton's car was burnt and that he had been killed. I had reached Britain and was staying with a very nice old Scottish couple, Reverend Forest and his wife Betty, with whom Orton had spent Christmas during his studies. The morning papers were usually on the breakfast table, but that particular day there were no papers and it struck me that something was wrong. Then their eldest son rushed in:

'Have you seen the awful news from Nyasaland?'

'What?' I wanted to know, but the parents looked sternly at him.

'Oh, nothing, I just got excited', he mumbled.

We ate breakfast, but as I was helping Reverend Forest with the dishes, Mrs Forest asked me to come with her.

'Let me just finish here', I said.

'No, Vera my dear, you must come now.'

She made me sit and then she knelt down like an African, touched my hand, and said:

'Vera, I'm sorry. . . .' Before she could finish I asked:

'Is my husband dead?'

'No, he's not dead.'

'Then what happened?'

'They say that Banda's people have burned his car.'

'Oh, my God, he's dead!'

'No, Vera, please calm down, maybe it's just the car.'

'No, he must have been inside it. Oh my God, he's dead.'

We immediately called some of Orton's good friends in London, who also did not know if Orton had survived and would try to find out from the Governor. They called Glyn Jones and he confirmed the story about the car, but he had also heard that Orton had been seen catching a boat somewhere on the lake, and promised to call back as soon as he knew what had happened.

The next couple of days were agonising, but people were very supportive. Professor Kitton of the Law Department and Mr Holland, who were great friends of Orton, arranged that I could start my term the following week, although my financial situation was suddenly very uncertain.

Orton had walked throughout the night and reached somewhere near Mount Mulanje, where he had laid down and slept on the side of the road. In the morning he had asked a man on a bicycle to take a note to my uncle and Rose's husband, Edwin Chiwambo, who was District Commissioner in nearby Chiradzulu.

'I'm here. I'm very tired. Can you come and collect me?' Orton wrote, and Edwin rushed to pick him up.

It was very dangerous for Rose and Edwin to keep Orton in their house, but he managed to shift to a hideout in David Rubadiri's mother's house in a small village on the other side of Blantyre. Orton's old friend David Rubadiri, whose wife had been my cellmate in Salisbury during the emergency, was now Malawi's UN Ambassador in New York. He had resigned in sympathy with the ministers and in disgust at having to vote for Dr Banda's pro-South African line in the UN assembly. His old mother gave Orton refuge until Chipembere and Chisiza found him and took him to Chipembere's stronghold in Mangotchi. From Mangotchi he hid in a ferryboat and finally reached Nkatha Bay. It was his home and nobody could harm him there. They had begun to mourn his death and were very pleased to see him back alive. Finally the Governor was also informed and called to tell us that Orton was safe.

A Treacherous Attack in State House

Dr Banda approached Governor Glyn Jones.

'Things are bad. I would very much like Orton Chirwa to come here so we can discuss recent developments and find out what to do. This is bad for our country.'

Glyn Jones still trusted Banda and sent a radio message to the District Commissioner in Nkatha Bay, which was brought to Orton's village. Orton called the local MCP committee.

'Now look, I was almost killed and now the Governor wants

me to go to meet Banda and I don't know why. What should I do?'

'You cannot refuse, when you don't know the message Banda has for you. You'd better go and sort things out', they argued.

'But I might be killed', Orton said.

'The risk is there, but we need to know what Dr Banda and the Governor have in mind.'

'Okay, I'm not afraid' – and off he went with a clear mandate from his constituency.

He was put up at Glyn Jones's own residence.

'Banda is very displeased with this situation', Glyn Jones told him. 'It's bad for the country. He wants to talk to you and I fully agree that the two of you should meet.'

'But I'm afraid that Dr Banda might have sinister motives for calling me here', Orton said. ' I barely escaped in Thondwe. They wanted to kill me.'

'No, no', Glyn Jones assured, 'Banda's is all right now. He's very apologetic.'

Orton agreed to a meeting the following morning. He went with a high-ranking European civil servant, Peter Hewings, but when they reached the gates of Dr Banda's residence the guards started to make trouble.

'Who are you to come here? We're going to beat you up. Open the door! Open the door!' they yelled, and hammered on the car.

Orton and Hewings went back. Glyn Jones phoned Dr Banda:

'What is all this? You want to meet Orton Chirwa and yet you can't even control your own bodyguards!'

'Oh, I'm so sorry', Dr Banda apologised, 'I didn't know. They must have acted on their own. It won't happen again.'

The next day they went again. There was nobody at the gate and they entered the house. Then Dr Banda came. That was his way. He never received visitors. They always ended up receiving him in his own house.

'Mr Chirwa', Dr Banda started, 'I talked to the Governor

because this situation is bad for our country. I have called you so we can discuss this issue.'

'That's very good. This situation is indeed very bad and it might become worse', Orton agreed. 'The others have left but Chipembere and Chisiza are still in the country. I think we should include those two in our talks.'

But the President refused:

'No, I don't want to talk to Chipembere and Chisiza!'

'It's not a matter of you and me discussing this situation. This concerns all of us and since they are still here, we should all meet', Orton insisted.

The leader got angry.

'Who do you think you are? You people! Wherever you go I'm going to hunt you down. You probably think I'm old and am going to die soon, but I can tell you, all of you will finish before I do!'

'Well, I refuse to talk to you like this. This is not a quarrel between you and me. It concerns us all', Orton said, and left.

When he opened the door, the guards were over him. A fat man, whom we knew very well from the League of Malawi Youth and who was now a leader of the Young Pioneers, hit Orton very hard. He fell to the ground and they started kicking him. Hewings tried to stop them, but they were too many. Orton looked up from the floor and saw Dr Banda peeping through the door. He heard him laugh. Then Kadzamira came:

'Stop it! You are killing Chirwa!' she yelled, 'He is the one who made you what you are. Stop!'

And they stopped. Orton was forever grateful to Kadzamira after that. Every time someone complained about her, he defended her:

'That woman saved my life', he always said.

Hewings managed to get hold of him, carried him to the car and drove back to the Governor's house. They were afraid that things would get out of hand if word came to the streets that

Orton had been beaten up. Luckily, Lady Glyn Jones was a nurse and she treated Orton's wounds. His clothes were all torn and he was in a miserable condition.

'I told you that Banda had sinister motives. I told you', Orton complained to the Governor, who was shocked.

'I didn't know. He's a dangerous person', Glyn Jones said and wanted to resign there and then.

He gave Orton a personal guard and sent him back home to Nkhata Bay.

'When people claim that I wanted to take over', Orton later said,' they should know that I had the opportunity that day. The whole army was there to escort me and protect me from the Young Pioneers. People just talk rubbish. If I had wanted to topple Banda and take government, I could have done it that day. But I didn't.'

A few days later, Chief Timbiri of Nkhata Bay was murdered in Zomba. Dr Banda had sent for the Chief because he wanted Timbiri to help him get rid of Orton. He is supposed to have offered Timbiri a high post as Native Authority in his area in return for the killing, but he did not know that Timbiri and Orton were close relatives.

'Orton is my cousin', Timbiri refused, 'I can't do that!'

When Timbiri was brought back after his meeting with the leader they did not take him all the way to his hotel. On Banda's orders he was left somewhere on the road and had to walk back to Hotel Manda in Zomba. It was dark and nobody knows what happened to Chief Timbiri. The next morning he was found dead.

The police claimed that they had conclusive evidence that Orton was involved. Rumour was spreading that Orton had killed the chief and at the burial Dr Banda ordered my uncle Edwin Chiwambo to attend the service as a civil servant and to state that Orton had murdered Timbiri. The relatives did not believe it. They knew that Orton was far from the scene, but had they believed in this rumour Orton, our children and the whole family would have been killed. The ground was burning under Orton's feet and he finally left for Tanzania – without the children.

5 Exile

'Why are my feet so swollen?' Nkhondo complained.

The children were still with Orton's parents. They had barely escaped the Young Pioneers, who came to raze Orton's ancestral village. The family had been warned and hid in a nearby riverbed. The Pioneers found the houses empty and burned everything down in frustration. They fled to my mother's village in Ngoniland. The Ngonis are formidable people and they took up their spears when the Young Pioneers came chasing after our children, but the Pioneers called the police and the whole village was arrested. My mother's two younger brothers were detained for almost a year after that, but our children got out under the Young Pioneers' noses.

They were on the run and it was hard for the two young boys. Zengani was still a toddler and was of course carried, but Nkhondo had to walk. He was exhausted and could not understand what was happening. Nyamazao and the others explained to him that Kamuzu Banda had chased us away. Dr Banda, remember, had named Nkhondo and his full name was Nkhondo Kamuzu Chirwa.

'I am no more Kamuzu! No more Kamuzu! Just Nkhondo. That's it. No more Kamuzu!' he cried. He was only three years old.

I was stuck in England and Orton had just arrived in Dar es Salaam. We had left Nyamazao with her aunt, Miriam, but Orton suddenly heard that Miriam had turned up in Lusaka – without

Nyamazao. Orton got very nervous and decided to rush back to Malawi and get the children out. He sent me a telegram:

'Going back to get the children. Would rather die together with them.'

That obviously disturbed me a lot. For two weeks I was in suspense. My friends tried to cheer me up and take me to the cinema, but I could not do anything.

'What's the use if they all die and I am left here alone', I said. I was sick with worry.

The Tanzanian President Julius Nyerere was very sympathetic to the ministers and the ones who came to Tanzania were immediately given refugee status, a house and a small stipend. Nyerere also gave Orton a Land Rover so he could drive back across the border and fetch the children.

They stealthily crossed into Malawi and Orton's brother, Duff Chirwa, got hold of a bicycle and cycled all the way to Mzimba district, where all the children, including Nyamazao, were hiding. Orton had given Duff some money and instructed him how to arrange for the children to buy false identity papers. He found the children and sent them on the road to the Tanzanian border, where Orton was waiting.

Orton's niece, Nyamanda, brought the children from Mzimba and the Pioneers were bothering her all the way.

'Why are you travelling with all these children? Are you trying to run away from something, little sister?' they quizzed her.

'No, no, I'm just going for a family visit', she insisted and they let her pass.

The children finally reached the border and were united with Orton. He sent me another telegram from Dar Es Salaam.

'Nyamazao and Company safely landed', it said and I started to eat again.

My tutor at the University College of London was very kind and she managed to raise some funds for me to go and see the family in the holiday break in 1965.

Things were bad. For the first time in our lives we were leading a very hard life. The allowances for the refugees had been reduced and Orton had to go to the small Arab shops in town and get beans, sugar and salt on credit. Life was tough. We barely had enough to live on and I found that my children had become very thin – especially Nkhondo and Zengani. But I had to go back and finish my studies.

I wrote my bar exams and my university final exams for the LLB in May 1966 and passed both. That was the joyful highlight of those tough years. I fought so hard to pass my LLB with honours in order to be able to finish my LLM in just one year. I also took a diploma in international law and passed my LLM in 1967. I had made it in spite of the extreme situation we had landed in, and graduated as the first woman lawyer in Southern Africa.

But how would I find the money to go back? I took temporary jobs and sorted mail in the post office, but it was not enough to buy the airfare to Dar es Salaam. Then a good friend, Margaret Benoit, came to my assistance and bought me a ticket. Finally, the family was united again.

Wondergirl

I arrived in Dar es Salaam on a Friday and the following Monday I started working as prosecuting state attorney in the Attorney General's chamber. Orton had already negotiated the position for me, which I happily accepted. He had also found work for himself as deputy commissioner in the land office, but the salary was quite small and we were still struggling to make ends meet.

The salary was low, but I was getting famous. The Tanzanian government made a figurehead out of me, because I was a married woman and a mother of five who had a unique career in a man's world. I was often on the radio and in magazines personifying progress for African women, and many Tanzanian women's organisations offered me jobs and board memberships.

The South African magazine *Drum* did a feature on me: one picture showed me cooking with my children, while in another I was transformed into a courtroom superhero, complete with wig and cape. The heading of the article was 'Wondergirl', which amused Orton a lot. It became his favourite pet name for me after that.

The Attorney General was satisfied with my work and appointed me as legal adviser to the inner Cabinet. It was an unusually confidential post to give to a woman and a foreigner, and I came to hear a lot of state secrets that I could not even reveal to Orton.

I won most of my cases, because I worked hard and prepared myself well for the hearings. The Tanzanian defence lawyers were not used to that. They often met their clients the same day they were to appear in court and they were not briefed properly. The judges were British and they were very strict on evidence and procedure. I mastered that well, but the defence fumbled and failed more often than not.

At a gathering for the legal community the Vice-President, Mr Kawave, made a speech and praised my work.

'We are very proud of Mrs Chirwa', he said. 'She knows her law and she knows her work.'

I was very proud – a woman, a refugee and a foreigner being praised by the Vice-President. All in all, those first few years in Tanzania were very rewarding for me professionally, but the family was struggling.

President Nyerere made explicit policies to ensure that refugees were treated as Tanzanian citizens and that our rights were protected. But refugees are always discriminated against and we were no exception.

Orton and I managed very well in our jobs, but the children

faced a lot of trouble in school. They were called *akimbisi*, a very derogatory name for refugees, and whenever they to had sit pass exams or shift to another school they were put in a foreigners' category behind the native Tanzanians.

Nyamazao was fortunate. She did so well in school that her British headmistress took a special interest in her and helped us to find a good school, while I was still in London studying law. Virginia was less fortunate and in the end Orton had to write to a friend and relative of ours, who was Minister of Education in Zambia, and ask him to help out with Virginia's education. He found a reasonable boarding school for her outside Lusaka and we had to send her there.

Fumbani was worst off. The doors were shut and the Tanzanians claimed that all schools were full. Orton tried to teach him at home for over two years, but it was hard for a young boy not to be in school. Soon Nkhondo and Zengani reached schooling age and we did not know whom to turn to for help.

But we were lucky. The head of the East African Community had heard about my work. The East African Community had offices in the three member states – Kenya, Uganda and Tanzania – and they were looking for a new legal counsel. They wrote to the Attorney General and offered me a job. However, I heard nothing about it. By accident I ran into a young lawyer who worked for the Community and whom I had coached in court.

'Oh, Mrs Chirwa, it's very good to hear that you are joining us at the Community', he said.

'The Community?', I was quite puzzled. 'I haven't applied for a job at the Community. . . .'

'No, no, the Council wrote to the Attorney General. Haven't you seen the letter?'

I had not and went straight to the Attorney General.

'I understand you have a letter for me from the East African Community', I said.

Vera Chirwa, called to the bar in 1966

Courtesy of Vera Chirwa

'Oh yes, as a matter of fact I have', he said. 'Do you want it?'

'Of course I want it! It's my letter.'

He handed it to me and it was indeed an offer of a position as legal counsel to the Community.

'Well, but we can't afford to lose you from this office', he said, 'and you are probably being posted in Arusha. Mr Chirwa wouldn't like that. You should rather be grateful that we have given you such a good job here in the chamber.'

I had always thought of him as a decent man and was quite surprised to see this side.

'This is a personal matter between my husband and me. It for us to decide, where I'm going to work, sir', I said – and marched out.

Orton was delighted. We were struggling with the school fees and wanted to send Nyamazao to India to finish her secondary schooling. The salary at the Community was three times higher than what I was getting as a prosecutor. I took the job. The Attorney General's behaviour had left little doubt in my mind, but I welcomed the change in many ways. No matter how seasoned a prosecutor I became, I continued to feel terrible when winning cases that ended in death penalties. I didn't like playing a part in sending people to the gallows and looked forward to moving out of the hangman's shadow. I started in 1973 and was posted in Dar es Salaam for the next three years.

Meat for the Crocodiles

In 1974 my younger brother Wishart Chirwa died in a road accident in Zambia, where he lived. I went to the burial and met my family for the first time in ten years. My father and my sister Chris came from Malawi. The funeral was swarming with Malawian agents. They mingled with the mourners in order to eavesdrop on my family and me. My father and I hardly dared to meet, but we had to exchange condolences. He stayed overnight at his brother's house and I met him there.

Chris and our father were arrested and interrogated immediately after their return to Malawi.

'You went to plot with your daughter', they said to my father. 'You are cooperating with these rebels.'

'They are not rebels to me', my father calmly said. He was a very firm man. 'They are my blood. Vera is my daughter and Orton is my son. If they came here this very minute I wouldn't hesitate to entertain them.'

'We'll tell Kamuzu', they threatened him. 'You'll not live through the night.'

'You tell him. Go ahead, tell him', my father said.

They kept him for three months.

Chris was let out shortly after the arrest. It was so obvious that she was not a politician, but they threatened her anyway. The entire family was suffering. My closest relatives failed to get jobs and were not allowed to enter good schools and universities. It was sad.

But the whole country was suffering. Dr Banda and his government created a reign of terror in Malawi and all dissidents, critics or influential people who got in their way were dealt with ruthlessly. It was a recurrent theme in the leader's thundering speeches that his enemies would end up as 'meat for the crocodiles'. We heard that MPs had laughed hysterically when he cracked jokes in Parliament in 1973 and referred to his former enemies in that infamous metaphor. The worst of it, of course, was that his cruel jokes seemed to be based on the literal truth. There were rumours of people disappearing and being taken to secret camps where they were tortured and thrown to the crocodiles in Shire River.

Refugees crossed the borders in flocks and Orton was often called to check and vouch for Malawians who sought political asylum in Tanzania. There were many undercover agents among them and the Tanzanian government wanted Orton's opinion on the credibility of their stories.

Orton had formed an exile movement in the late 1960s, shortly after I returned from London. It was called the Malawian Freedom Movement, MAFREMO. We felt a need to organise the exiles and coordinate our effort to topple Dr Banda and transform Malawi into a multi-party democracy. We consulted the Malawian community in Tanzania but had to be quite discreet. The Tanzanian government did not allow foreigners to form political movements, fearing retaliation by their home countries, and so MAFREMO had to be an underground movement.

We called the first general meeting in a hotel in Dar es Salaam and many people came, but some of our trusted and close friends did not show up. It came as a surprise to us that many of them were already part of another exile organisation, the Socialist League of Malawi (LESOMA), formed by Attati Mpakati in Mozambique with an explicitly militant and socialist approach to the fight against Dr Banda.

It turned out that one of our closest friends in Tanzania, my cousin's husband – whom Orton had asked to become secretary general of MAFREMO – was already secretary general of LESOMA. Orton was very puzzled.

'Why didn't you tell us? We could have joined forces. Why let us embark on the formation of MAFREMO, if you were already involved in another organisation? We should work together!'

But they were quite evasive and only wanted to focus on young people. They even tried to entice Nyamazao without telling us, but she refused. Some of our other friends also began to act strangely and we felt they were not being straight with us. They too were senior members of LESOMA.

We formed MAFREMO anyway. Orton was elected president and I was unanimously elected treasurer. People were sure that a woman was the right person to take care of the finances. We started our work and the movement became very popular. We wrote to fellow Malawian exiles, held meetings and conventions, and tried to coordinate the political battle against Dr Banda.

Securing the welfare and education of our children continued to be an uphill task. In Zambia there were considerably better opportunities to get them into good schools without all these problems, and Orton and I took a difficult decision. I applied for a job as lecturer in law at the University of Zambia. They offered me the chair as the first woman to teach law at a university in Southern Africa and we decided that I should take the two youngest boys with me to Lusaka. Orton had opened a private law practice in Dar es Salaam and wanted to stay – at least for some years – and so in 1977 I moved again.

6 *We Have Got You Today*

'We Have Got You Today'

We had travelled too long and too far off the main road, criss-crossing along narrow muddy trails in the dark. There was a car parked in front of us in the middle of the road, and our driver was honking, blast after blast.

'Maybe he has just gone to relieve himself in the bush', I thought, but our driver got out.

'Let me go and check why this man has stopped right here on the road', he said.

Suddenly, the door on my right was opened and there were flashlights in our eyes. Someone reached over me and hit Orton straight in the face.

'Why are you hitting me?' Orton yelled, and the man said:

'Yes, we have got you today!'

The doors were torn open and they came out of the bush from all sides, dressed in camouflage uniforms like soldiers. Before I could do anything, they were on me.

When I go a meeting, I am always well dressed. That night I was wearing my hat, my golden turquoise earrings with a matching necklace, some expensive gold bangles, my watch and so on. I do not know what happened to Orton and Fumbani, but the people who swamped the car were certainly struggling to strip me of everything valuable. My necklace, my watch, my hat, even my shoes, but although they were tearing and tearing they could not get the bangles off. I was dragged out and thrown on the ground, with my head under the car. One of them kicked me in the stomach and I was bleeding and passing motion. It was total chaos, and I could not hear what they were saying. They pushed me and handcuffed me, put shackles on my legs, blindfolded me with some sort of tight, rubber band and threw me into another vehicle.

'You are hurting me. It's too tight. Take it off', I told them, 'what can I see at night?', but they just left it there:

'If you see anything we are going to kill you!'

It was Christmas Eve 1981. Who were these people?

I had become quite ill by the end of 1981 and finally decided to go to Scotland for a thorough medical check-up. It turned out that I had a serious case of thyroid gland deficiency, and when I returned to Lusaka it was so bad that I had to go back to Orton in Dar es Salaam for a month's rest.

While I was in Scotland MAFREMO had held a convention in Mbeya, close to the border between Tanzania and Malawi. Delegates had come from many countries – America, Britain, Zambia and so on. They were all MAFREMO members and refugees from the Banda regime. Some delegates had even come from Malawi thereby establishing MAFREMO as an underground movement within Malawi itself. It was very successful and they had decided that Orton should hold another meeting in Zambia close to the Malawian border to meet more members from Malawi. After a month in Dar es Salaam I was ready to go back to the university, and since Orton was on his way to this meeting, we decided to go together and to take our son, Fumbani, along as well. But the problem was transport. It was Christmas and everything was booked. All flights, trains and even the good buses were full: people now tell us that this was a bad omen. Since we were running late we had to take an ordinary public bus, and we were on the road for a week. The bus kept breaking down and we had to wait for them to repair it. Sometimes we even found ourselves on the road pushing it. It was terrible.

When we finally reached Lusaka, Orton only had two or three days left before he would have to attend a High Court session, and we rushed straight to the border town of Chipata where the meeting was to be held. Our daughter, Virginia, lived in Chipata. She had invited us for Christmas the previous year, but I had not gone because of my illness. Now Virginia had extended the invitation again, but Orton only had time to spend an afternoon at her house, where the organisers of the MAFREMO meeting were to pick him up.

The organiser of the meeting was a man named Mwananku. He had attended the MAFREMO convention in Mbeya and offered to host the meeting. Mwananku was a Malawian, but he had a large farm on the Zambian side of the border, where the Malawian delegates could meet. Mwananku was late. It was getting dark and we thought he had given up on us.

When he finally came, Orton stressed that we did not have much more time available, but Mwananku answered that the people who had come to hear him were already gathered and waiting. Since Orton wanted to return the same evening, I thought I might as well join him. Fumbani was to accompany his father to the meeting and we all set off in Mwananku's car.

Mwananku's farm was somewhere off the main road that runs from Chipata to the border post, and we drove deep into the villages along some very narrow roads. At a certain place Mwananku wanted to stop and collect something, and we had to wait for a new car because the driver, who was hired, apparently had to go back. We waited and waited. Orton and Mwananku were discussing politics and I was telling Fumbani about my last couple of months running from one medical examination to the other.

There were many rumours about Banda sending terrorists across the borders and as time slipped by I grew slightly suspicious.

'Why are we delaying like this?' I asked Fumbani, 'I hope we are not being tricked! Suppose they kill us, and no one even knows where we are.'

'Oh, Mama, don't talk about such things!' both Orton and Fumbani said, and we all laughed at my fears.

Finally the new car came, but our journey seemed endless. Every time we saw some lights I asked:

'Is this the place? Is this the place?' and Mwananku kept saying that we were almost there.

Orton did not seem unduly anxious and was busy talking to Mwananku about the meeting.

After some time, we stopped and greeted a large group of people, who were lined up along the road. We shook hands with them and they were very excited. Mwananku said it was some of the delegates and that we were very close now. We got into the car again and drove a short distance before the driver suddenly stopped and hooted and honked at that car parked in the middle of the road. I do not know whether our driver was part of what happened next, because I never saw him again after the kidnappers attacked us. We were beaten, tied, blindfolded and thrown into separate vehicles.

The vehicle I was in started to move. My panties were full of blood and faeces and I felt terrible.

'Stop and let me go and pass motion outside', I implored, but they refused.

There were a lot threats and abusive talk during that drive.

'Let's stop here and rape her', someone said at one point.

I was very frightened and started praying:

'My God, don't allow these dirty people to touch me. Please God protect me from these ruffians. Don't let them touch me.' I repeated this again and again in my heart.

Suddenly, we stopped. The driver did not know where to go, and someone in the back said:

'Let's take them where we always take them.'

'Yah,' someone else said, 'let's torture them first. Let's take them there.'

I just kept praying. Prayer has saved me many times and the driver insisted on getting instructions from a superior. I heard the door slam, and after some time he came back.

'I've been told to take them to Kanengo', he said, and the others were very disappointed:

'Oh, no! Why is that? What's so special with her?' But the driver insisted on going straight to Kanengo, and while the others were murmuring in the back I was thanking God for not letting them take me to that other place of torture.

Kanengo

I thought we were still in Zambia, in the hands of Zambian bandits. There was no Kanengo in Malawi when we left, and I had never heard of this place. We stopped and I was taken up some steps, then through a door. Still blindfolded and in chains, I sensed that I was now in a very small room. Then I heard them talking outside:

'She has to be searched.'

'But it's past midnight; all the wardresses have gone home.'

'Oh, is it past midnight? Okay then, call the wife of sergeant so-and-so.'

They were speaking a form of Nyanja, but the accents in Zambia and Malawi are slightly different, and I was beginning to wonder whether this one was actually a Malawian accent. The ladies – two of them – came to search me and I was ordered to take off my panties, full of blood and faeces. I felt sorry for them. They were just laywomen, warders' wives, what did they know?

Since they had taken me in a separate car, I thought I was the only one alive and that Orton and Fumbani had been killed, but I was praying for them:

'Wherever they are, my Lord, protect them as you are protecting me.'

Next morning they took me out. My face was swollen from the beating and my eyes were so full of blood that I could hardly see, but somebody held my arm and led me outside to stand in the shade. Then I heard the chains – cling, cling. It was Fumbani, chained on hands and feet like me, and he was alive. Later Orton came out too. They had stolen his tie and jacket and he was just in his trousers with a torn shirt. He looked really dishevelled.

'Oh, what is all this?' Orton said, but the guards barked at him:

'No talking to each other! Shut up or we'll shoot you.'

They paraded us up and down in the yard for some time and took us back inside, one by one.

The room where I had spent the night was some kind of store. It was so small that I could not even lie at full length on the floor. They kept me there for the next three months.

I was soon to learn that Kanengo was one of those secret places deep in the forest, out of sight, where people were hidden and killed during Banda's regime. The food was awful and my condition was deteriorating rapidly. My eyes were full of blood, I had high blood pressure, and my asthma and thyroid ailment were worse. I was close to death before they realised how bad a state I was in, but the medical assistant at Kanengo was a good man. He always sang hymns for me – I think he was a Seventh Day Adventist – and soon after the arrest he came to see me thrice a day. That man saved my life, as Kadzamira had saved Orton's.

Others were less gentle. Early on in my stay a senior police officer barged into the room in the middle of the night, scaring the wits out of me as they always strive to do.

'I have come here to see that you are happy and don't have any problems', he said.

'You see my condition? I am a patient, just out of hospital, and where are we? Why are we here?'

But that man was rude in a very underplayed way: 'Oh, you are in Kanengo, in Malawi. We have brought you back to your home. What were you doing in Tanzania?' he asked with a smile, and I started to realise the situation we were in.

We were not allowed to see each other, and I had no idea how Orton and Fumbani were doing. They put us together for about half an hour once, but we were not allowed to talk of the arrest or our conditions, and could just say 'I'm glad to see you' and things like that.

I got on well with the young policewoman who cleaned my room.

'We know you haven't done anything wrong', she said. 'You have been to Tanzania, but this is Malawi. It's how they do things here.'

She was a good girl. She even made an effort to kill all the mosquitoes in the room, so I could get a bit of rest. One day when she was cleaning I was standing outside and she told me that Orton and Fumbani were in the cells just down the corridor. I was thinking hard and fast on how to contact Fumbani, and I started to jump up and down, shouting:

'Bunyenye! Bunyenye!'

I was pretending to do exercises, but I was in fact calling out Fumbani's pet name, Bunyenye. I saw him climb up to the bars, trying to peep out, and in our local language I called:

'Are you okay?'

'Yah, Mama', he answered.

Then another, much less friendly wardress came along, and I had to stop:

'Are you doing exercises?' she wanted to know.

'Yah, what can I do with these chains', I answered her, but at least I had found out that my son was well.

I also found out that they would take Orton past my room when he was going to bathe. I heard his chains ringing day after day, and climbed up to see who it was. It was Orton, but how could I speak to him? There were other people among the Kanengo staff who sympathised with us, and someone must also have told Orton where I was, because suddenly he started singing on his way to the bath. As he was passing my room he would sing a song in our local language with a secret message to me:

'Don't worry, we are going home', he sang in his deep voice, 'Dr Banda has found out that we did not come here to kill him, and has asked us to choose whether we want to go to Zambia or straight back to Dar es Salaam.'

He sang like that every time they took him to his bath.

After some time the Inspector General of Police and a few other senior officers came to Kanengo to see us and the three of us were called into an office to meet them. They were very pleasant and told us that we were to go home soon.

'They are coming tomorrow', Orton sang to me a few days later. 'They say Banda wants to show us the development. Banda is saying that before I go, I have to see all the developments that I always accused him of failing to introduce, especially in the North. We are going to see developments tomorrow, but I don't know what they are. I don't see any', Orton sang.

The following morning I heard Orton leave. He was chatting and laughing with the officers – he always got on well with them – and they took off in cars. They left Fumbani and me behind, and I became very suspicious.

'They are going to kill him', I thought.

Around noon they picked me up as well. I had to go and sign for my things and see that everything was there. The jewellery, of course, was not. They put Fumbani and me in separate cars, and we drove off.

We reached a huge open prison. I had never seen an open prison before and was quite puzzled by all these people, who were obviously prisoners and yet were walking about in the open. We stopped and they took Fumbani to an office building of some kind, but my car continued. The suspicion grew serious.

'We are being separated and they are slaughtering us one by one. Now they are taking me somewhere to die. This is our fate. Today they are going to kill us all.'

I was thinking like that in the car, driving away and leaving Fumbani behind. But I kept quiet.

I was taken to an airfield and boarded a small police plane. There was no conversation whatsoever with the guards. They never tell you where you are going or even talk to you. You just have to bear it. You may suspect this or that, but there is nobody to answer your questions. I saw the lake and thought we were going to Likoma Islands, but then again I kind of sensed we were heading north. In fact, we landed in Mzuzu, but I did not know where we were at that time, and again a police vehicle took me to some building or other. I heard the guards say, 'Let us wait for them here', and after some very agonising moments I realised that I was going to meet the head of police security. He was very pleasant and said that Orton had wanted me to join him.

'Mr Chirwa was not budging. When he discovered that we hadn't brought you, he insisted. He doesn't want to see these developments alone', the police officer said, 'So, although we are late we had to bring you. Dr Banda told us to take you back to Chipata, but I'm not sure we can reach there today. We'll try, but I'm not sure.'

He escorted me to another police vehicle, where Orton was waiting.

'Where is Fumbani? I want my son to be with me', Orton said.

I told him that Fumbani had been taken to an open prison, and we drove off, but we did not reach Chipata.

'Oh, we're so sorry,' they said, 'but the plane has no lights. We can't fly you back, so tonight you have to stay at Lilongwe Prison.'

So we went there.

The Kangaroo Court

After Lilongwe we were taken to Chichiri Prison. I was put in a large dormitory-type cell meant for at least 50 people, but I was not allowed to see or speak to anyone, so they removed all the other prisoners and left me there all alone. The officer in charge was sympathetic to my situation and ordered the wardresses to sleep inside the cell with me. They really complained:

'Why should we be locked up with this woman as if we too are prisoners?'

'She's all alone', he insisted. 'She can't sleep in a big room like this under these circumstances.'

The following day the trial started. The police claimed that we had come back to Malawi to kill Dr Banda. They claimed that they had intercepted our murderous plans and caught us inside Malawi (rather than abducting us from a foreign country). On 29 July 1982 we were charged with treason. We were tried in a Traditional Court, consisting of three chiefs and a magistrate who was there to guide the chiefs in matters of law. The chairman was Chief Nazombe and the magistrate was a young man called Tweya.

The Traditional Court was by then a part of the legal system Dr Banda had developed to do away with political opponents under the semblance of 'legal process'. We immediately asked for legal representation, but they refused. We were not allowed to have lawyers – but that was just the beginning of the farcical rulings and proceedings of this 'kangaroo court'.

We began by disputing the jurisdiction of the court. We had

Times

Golden Qua

THURSDAY 29 JULY, 1982   REGISTERED AT THE G.P.O. AS A NEWSPAPER

Couple charged with treason

FIVE NAMED ACCOMPLICES

Blantyre, Wednesday

ORTON Chirwa, a former Cabinet Minister who was among those who fled the country in late 1964 after a Cabinet crisis, and his wife, Vera, this morning appeared before the Southern Regional Traditional Court at Soche in Blantyre jointly charged with treason.

Both Orton, 63, and Vera, 49, pleaded "not guilty" in a packed court before a five-man panel of judges whose Chairman is Chief Nazombe of Mulanje. A growing number of people outside the courtroom followed the proceedings from loudspeaker relays.

The charge alleges that Orton Edgar Ching'oli Chirwa and Vera Orton Chirwa during the month of April, 1977 and on divers other days thereafter up to and including December

TIMES REPORTER

24, 1981 at several places outside Malawi, namely in Tanzania and in Zambia, being citizens of the Republic of Malawi or persons owing allegiance thereto, together with Winston Msowoya, Boyd Kamanga, John Mgayi, Henry Chikoti and Mackenzie Chirwa and with other persons unknown, prepared, endeavoured or conspired to overthrow the lawfully constituted Government of the Republic of Malawi by force or other unlawful means."

Of the charge, Orton,

Orton Chirwa (left) and wife Vera Chirwa (right) in the Southern Regional Traditional Court, Soche. —Picture by Daily Times

speaking in English, replied: "I deny the charge, my lord. It's not true."

Agreeing that he was 63 years old, Orton, however, refused that Chijere was his home. "My lord, my home is in Dar-es-Salaam," he said, adding that Chijere Village was a home he left "a long time ago" in 1940 and that his last home in Malawi was in Limbe.

Also agreeing that he

"originally" came from Traditional Authority Timbiri in Nkhata Bay, Orton also affirmed that his last address in Tanzania was Box 3132 in Dar-es-Salaam.

Vera, initially replying in vernacular but later switching to English, refused that she came from Masasa Village in Nkhata Bay District.

Continued on Page 9

Tight budget

HARARE, Wednesday

ZIMBABWE Finance Minister Bernard Chidzero is expected to announce modest tax increases and

READ INTE

If your funds are not earning

Front page of *The Daily Times* announcing the trial
of Orton and Vera Chirwa, 29 July 1982

Courtesy of *The Daily Times*

read the Evidence and Procedure Act, which stated that a person tried with treason had to be a resident of Malawi.

'We are Malawians,' we argued, 'this is our country and we are proud of it. We are citizens of Malawi, but we are not residents here. We are residents of Tanzania. Accordingly, we cannot be tried by this court. It has no jurisdiction over us.'

That gave them something to think about and the chiefs retired into their small room. When they came back they said:

'No, we have the right to try you. It has been discussed with the head of this country and he has put us here to try troublesome people like you!'

So, they started trying us, and we kept challenging the court. Initially, they did not allow us to refer to each other's cases. I was stopped every time I used the word 'we', because they did not want us to start defending each other. In fact, they tried to turn me against my own husband and make me say that Orton had misled me, but I saw through that very easily:

'How can I not talk about things touching upon my husband's case, when you have charged us together? You have charged us together and if there are things that concern him they concern me.'

They could not get around that, and we established that we could defend each other.

It was obvious that they wanted Orton. He was the one that they had planned to abduct and possibly even kill in connection with the MAFREMO meeting. They had not expected Fumbani and me to be there as well. We were there by accident and I am sure it changed the course of events dramatically. It protected Orton, especially, during the trial, and I really defended him well. Had it been a proper court, he would have been acquitted, but we knew that he had already been convicted.

The witnesses were all policemen. Not a single witness was a civil person, and there was no evidence. According to the British procedure, which was supposed to be the foundation of that court, it is up to the prosecutor to prove the guilt of the accused person by cogent evidence beyond reasonable doubt. It is called the adversarial system of justice. Instead they tried to use the trial to extract evidence from us, following an inquisitorial approach, but we protested:

'What is this? The inquisitorial system of justice is used in France. It's not the system we use here. You can't do this.'

The prosecution did not make sense at all. When you want to prove a treason charge you obviously need to produce accomplices, witnesses with whom the accused has been conspiring, but they only called police officers. One of the worst examples was Mr Chalila, who was head of the Criminal Investigation Department. After this witness had been led by the prosecutor, Orton was going to cross-examine him. Chalila was first of all an investigating officer, and they wanted to prove that Orton had written a certain letter, but Chalila was also called as an expert witness on handwriting.

'I have never heard of a person who is investigating a case concerning the writing of a letter being called both as a witness in the case and as a witness evaluating the evidence as a handwriting expert. This man is prejudiced!'

Chalila was abusive. He called Orton stupid, which really hurt me. When it's my turn, I am going to give him hell, I thought. But Orton calmly carried on:

'What have I to do with this? The question is, isn't there another handwriting expert?' Then he started to go through Chalila's 'expert' evidence, tearing it apart.

During my cross-examination, Chalila's rudeness continued, but I ignored him:

'You must answer the questions I put to you. When Accused Number One' – that was what they called Orton – 'asked you this question, you ridiculed him, but isn't it correct that you later on used exactly the same argument in your own evidence? So, I am asking you, how clever are you really?'

He got increasingly confused and abusive: 'After all, I win cases here, all cases!' he hissed, and mentioned some of the other famous Malawian political trials like Muwalu's and Chakuamba's. 'I won all of them, and I pity you that you will never see the outside again.'

That hurt.

'What kind of witness are you? You are making a judgement here, Sir. You are the prosecutor, the investigating officer, the expert witness and now also the judge?'

'I don't care. All Malawians know that you came here to kill Dr Banda and everybody else!' On he went, but at least I had humiliated him.

The case dragged on for more than nine months. They had no evidence, but had to finish what they had started and could not cut the trial short. Since it was clear that they had already found us guilty, we decided to turn our defence against them in another way. Malawians did not know what had happened during the Cabinet Crisis that had driven us into exile. They did not know their rights, and we wanted to take this opportunity to tell the people the real story about their country. The trial was very well publicised. They had put loudspeakers outside and there was a lot of press coverage. It was an excellent platform and people were supporting us. That was Dr Banda's problem. I am sure he had expected us to talk about ourselves during the proceedings and they tried their best to pit us against each other, but we turned that upside down. Orton would ask:

'Who formed the Malawi Congress Party?'

They knew very well that it was Orton, but people were supposed to think that Dr Banda had formed the MCP, and they could not answer. We made it difficult for them and they often just had to resort to answers like:

'Don't ask us stupid questions!'

People gathered outside the court in large numbers and cheered us on. The chiefs were completely useless. The Chairman, Nazombe, was sleeping all the time and only woke up to exclaim:

'Court adjourned! Court adjourned!'

So the audience in the courtroom and the people outside started booing him, even though many were arrested. In that sense we really enjoyed the trial. We had the support of our fellow Malawians.

At the same time we were suffering badly in custody. We were not allowed to see each other or to have any visitors and we were maltreated, especially Orton. They feared that people would riot and demonstrate if we were driven through the streets of Zomba and Blantyre during the day and we were always taken to court early in morning and brought back to the prison at night. I was kept in Zomba Prison at that time and Orton was in Mkuyu. One night, when they dropped me and escorted me into the entrance building at Zomba, they took Orton along as well. I was happily surprised and hoped we might have one of our few and cherished opportunities to talk together. They made me sit on a bench, which was unusual, and I was thinking that they were giving me special treatment just to irritate Orton. He was made to squat on the floor beside me. He was very thin. His lips were red and his bones were showing. He looked like a boy. Immediately, the officer in charge started poking him with a stick:

'Come on, get up, get up!' but he was so weak that he was about to fall all the time and the officer just poked and poked him.

Orton was a man and he hauled himself up.

'Get out, get out! Let's go!' the officer yelled.

I was so hurt. They had brought my husband there to be humiliated in front of his wife.

'Why are they maltreating the man who brought freedom to this country? He risked a lot, my husband, and now this. . . .'

The Black Bag

The trial was still on and we were tearing the witnesses apart one by one. It was even funny at times. One witness was the head of the mobile police force, Mr Likaomba, who was a typical male chauvinist. After he had been led by the prosecutor and cross-examined by Orton, it was my turn.

'I don't answer questions from a woman', he said.

He thought that he was going to make fun of me, but the stupid man did not know that I was a woman activist. As a barrister you are trained to carry yourself in a very proper manner and I continued unmoved by his rudeness.

'Sir, you have to answer my question.'

'I can't answer a question from a woman.'

'So you fail to answer my question?'

'I can't fail a question put by a woman.'

'Then answer.'

'I don't answer que. . .'

'Now, look!' I said. 'You think you are being rude to me, but you are in fact being rude to the bench, you see, rude to those gentlemen sitting over there. You are being rude to the court in general. So, will you answer my question?'

When he went on with his insults, I said:

'Sir, you look around. Do you see these policemen there? If you are not going to answer my question, I will ask the court to adjourn and these policemen will arrest you. There's an empty cell between my husband and me, where you are going to be put, and later on you are going to come here and be tried for contempt of the court and you are going to be convicted and you will be in that cell with us. So, can you answer my question?'

I looked him straight in the face with my right hand on my waist and people outside were laughing. They were arrested for cheering, of course, but when he started answering my questions people went: 'Ooooooooh!' That is how you defeat a man who looks down on women.

The most famous police blunder concerned my black handbag. Today, people still make jokes when I carry a black bag. The police claimed to have found a number of incriminating documents in it that proved we were coming to Malawi to kill and overthrow Dr Banda. The documents, of course, were forged and planted there. They brought the bag and its alleged contents to the courtroom as evidence, and I immediately spotted their mistake. A police officer went through the items one by one, including the documents, and presented the evidence to the chiefs.

When it was my turn to cross-examine him, I asked him to do it again. Slowly and thoroughly he went through all the items and explained how they had found them in my bag.

'And you found these items in the bag?' I asked him.

'Yes.'

'Including these documents you refer to?'

'Yes.'

'And you are sure that you found all of these items in that bag?'

'Yes, all of them were there.'

'Then I ask you kindly to put all the items back into the bag.'

He went to the table where the things were displayed and started to stuff them in. Of course, only half the contents fitted into the bag. . . .

Finally, the case was concluded. It was still dark when they picked us up early in the morning for the judgement. The magistrate was summing up and discrediting everything the police had said. He drew his conclusion:

'Mr Chirwa demolished the prosecutor's evidence, and we agree with him.'

We had defended ourselves so well that they actually had to admit that there was no cogent evidence, but we knew they wanted Orton. They had put a lot of work into it and we were still expecting his conviction.

'But there is not a shred of evidence against *you*', Orton said. 'You're going to be acquitted. You'll be just like Winnie Mandela.'

'I'm already more than Winnie Mandela,' I told him, 'and you can be sure I'll fight for you.'

There was no case against me, yet both of us were convicted and sentenced to death on 6 May 1983.

Although we were prepared for the worst, it was a big shock, especially for me. We appealed immediately.

The traditional court system was introduced after we had left Malawi and I did not know how it operated. I was certain that the appeal would go to the High Court, and I was confident that we would be acquitted in a proper trial. However, the appeal court was also a traditional court. Once again we were facing the chiefs. They just shifted the chairman. We realised there was no hope and I felt it in my stomach:

'My God, are you sure it's the chiefs again?' And they just said: 'Yes.'

The new chairman was Chief Mzukuzuku, from the north. Apparently, Dr Banda wanted Chief Mmbelwa to preside over the appeal, but he refused because we were related. In fact, Mzukuzuku was also a relative, my father's cousin and old friend, but he accepted the chair for the appeal. My father never spoke to him again. The appeal started in September 1983.

In the appeal it was a judge, and not a magistrate, who advised the chiefs. Again the case dragged on, but in February 1984 we received our final verdict. The judge summed up and they accepted all the evidence in Orton's case except for one particularly blatant lie. In my case, however, the court did not accept a single piece of evidence: yet I was convicted again. That was the judgement of the appeal court. As a lawyer you learn that when a judge is reading the judgement, you should not interfere. You cannot simply interrupt the judge and say: 'Hey, stop! I want to say something here!' But I did exactly that. Orton was a formal and very principled man and as I started to get up he tried to hush me.

'No, Vera you can't interrupt the judge.' But I insisted.

'You threw the evidence away, you disbelieved the lies of the police, and still you are using that same evidence to convict me. There is no evidence against me at all!'

They looked like fools. Chairman Mzukuzuku said:

'Court adjourned!' and they retired to their room.

The judge, who had taken the magistrate's place, now actually tried to uphold the law. Throughout the appeal, he had kept saying that we should never have been tried, and that it was wrong according to the Evidence and Procedure Act. When they came back, he said:

'I told the chiefs it was wrong', and there was a lot of confusion. He was sticking his neck out for us, and after the judgement he had to leave the country. 'All the time I have been saying that you should not have been tried by this court,' he continued, 'but the vote has to be respected and the majority has now convicted you like this. I'm going to write a minority judgement, and as you know you can always appeal.'

'To whom am I going to appeal?' I asked. 'This is the final court. Once you convict, I'm gone. Where can I appeal? It is now that you have to resolve it. Throw the case away, now, and I'll be acquitted.'

The judge repeated he had to accept the majority vote and the chiefs just said: 'We are here to convict all political prisoners.'

So I was convicted and both Orton and I were sentenced to death.

Usually, when a sentence is passed, the police take the prisoners away quickly, but in this case they were all mesmerised. Everyone was just sitting there, so I got up and took the stage, the political platform:

'Let me tell you something, people. See how our government is violating your rights. They kill you. We're here and we want to liberate you and we're not afraid to die for our people. I am very happy that I am here and when I die my blood will water the plants of Malawi so they can grow and gain in strength.'

Then the chief prosecutor ordered the police to take us away, but Orton, who was standing next to me, cut him off:

'Shut up, stooge! Let her talk!'

So I talked and talked, but they eventually gained the courage to lead us up the stairs of the court. At the top of the stairs I started discrediting the government again, and again Orton backed me up:

'Let her talk!'

'Let's go, madam,' my wardress was saying, 'please, let's go.' She was crying.

'Don't cry', I told her. 'Someone has to die for what we want to achieve. Someone has to die for the people. Don't cry.'

But they cried for us, so I said: 'Okay, we can go now.'

That was the final moment of the trial, and I enjoyed it. For a politician to have that kind of support – that was what I needed most of all.

As we were leaving, Orton said: 'Vera, let's forgive their weaknesses, their lies, Dr Banda – everybody. All those police and prison officers, who lied against us, let's forgive them. They didn't do it on purpose. They were afraid to lose their jobs. Jesus says we must forgive, so let's forgive them all.'

7 *The Will to Live*

'Vera, we are going to talk now. This is our chance', Orton insisted. 'Remember the stories you told me about the cancer patients in England?'

After the intensely powerful experience in the courtroom we found ourselves in a police car on the way back to prison with an execution hanging over our heads. Orton wanted me to remember a television programme about people suffering from cancer that I had seen during my last trip to England. The main character was a woman, told by the doctors that she would die within three months. But the woman had mustered an extraordinary will to live and was still alive three years later. The woman's inner strength had fascinated me and I had told Orton about her.

'This will to live is now for us to find. We have to have the will to live, Vera. We are going to be separated for God knows how long. We might die, they might execute us, but we have to have the will to live, to do exercises and to pray. We have to promise each other that. Okay?'

'Okay', I said and we started laughing together on the way back to prison.

The guards were puzzled:

'We have taken hardened criminals from the court who have tried to commit suicide after a death sentence, but you two are laughing away. What is this?'

Orton got off and was taken to the men's section. Over the next nine years I only saw him twice.

Cell Number 2

We reached the prison and I was suddenly very, very tired. We had not eaten since 3 o'clock in the morning, when they had picked us up for court. I asked the prison officers for some food.

'Mrs Chirwa, how can you ask for food right after a death sentence? You have not lost your appetite?' the officer asked.

'Don't you eat?' I asked him. 'I'm very hungry.'

The cooks had left for the day, but the officer promised to try and organise some food and drink.

More than 30 people escorted me to my cell. I was walking in the middle of this large group of police and prison officers and I decided to be slightly insubordinate and antagonise them a bit.

'I'm tired, I'm hungry and I'm condemned to death and I'll walk at my own pace', I told them, and walked very slowly.

It frustrated the guards – 'When are we going to reach her cell?' – but I kept my pace and sang 'O when the saints ...' to myself. Slowly, slowly to the rhythm: 'O Lord, I want to be in that number ... When the saints go marching in', step by step, in my chains, towards my cell.

The cell was fairly big. It was the small section of the prison, which was built for white prisoners during colonial days, but after independence white prisoners were mixed with Malawians and the 'White Section' was made into a Women's Ward. They put me in Cell Number 2 in a small block with four cells, but the three other cells were empty. The block was fenced in and they really made an effort to isolate me from the rest of the women prisoners.

There was something wrong with my chains and they sent someone to get another set. A senior officer from Prison Headquarters, Mr Chikwenembe, entered the cell with two other officers.

'Clear everything, take it out!' he shouted.

'Not the water. I want water', I protested. There was some water in a bucket and I was very thirsty.

'No, no, no, take it out! Everything! Out!'

He called a woman officer, who came in to put on the new chains. She must have fumbled a bit, because Chikwenembe got furious and stepped in:

'Ah, you are wasting our time here! We are tired. Come on!'

He pushed her away and chained me very tightly.

'Ah, please, you're hurting me!' I cried, but he did not care.

'Out, out everybody!' he yelled and they all left.

I was sitting there alone. The chains hurt my wrists and ankles terribly and I was still hungry and thirsty. It was a very hard moment for me.

'What is this? What is going to happen to me now?' I was thinking, but sleep came to me, sweet, sweet sleep.

When I woke up the chains had chafed my flesh. It was all swollen and there was blood on the cuffs. The officer in charge of the prison, Mr Mwale, came at 6 o'clock in the morning to check on me, as he would continue to do every morning for many years to come.

'How have you slept?' he asked me.

Chichewa had been introduced as the *lingua franca* in Malawi after Orton and I had escaped in 1964. I had spoken Swahili all the time in Tanzania and was not very good at Chichewa yet.

'How can I express myself so they really understand how hurt I am?' I wondered, and I tried my best in broken Chichewa:

'A big officer comes from the Headquarters and cruelly chains a woman. Here I am. See my wounds.'

My words happened to come out in a very moving way in Chichewa and the women guards dropped tears.

'I'm very sorry', Mr Mwale said. 'Why didn't you tell him it was too tight?'

'I told him three times, but he didn't care.'

'I'm sorry. I have tried to find some food for you, but the cooks have not arrived yet. Give her some water and some tea', he ordered.

'I don't want your water. I don't want your tea. I don't want your porridge. I don't want anything from you!' I cried.

'Okay, okay, we'll go', Mr Mwale said, and, turning to his junior officers, 'According to the rules she's supposed to be in chains, but as you can see this is too much. If a senior officer comes, I take full responsibility. Take the chains off her. I'll let you know when to put them back on. I'm going to call a doctor.'

They took the chains off me. He was a nice man, Mr Mwale, and I heard him give them instructions as they walked away:

'She's very upset now, but go and give her some porridge at around 10 o'clock and make sure she takes it. And you women stop crying! You are supposed to be prison officers. Stop that!'

I was eventually chained again and, despite Mr Mwale's and some of the other officers' genuine commitment to upholding a just and humane regime in the prison, the treatment was very bad. Orton and I were not allowed to see each other. We could have neither visitors, nor pen and paper, nor books. We could not receive letters or write to our relatives and loved ones. We were not allowed to talk to fellow prisoners or even to the guards. For the first couple of years I was under constant surveillance by two women guards who were supposed to watch over each other so that I was totally unable to speak to anybody at all. Of course, some guards were less strict than others.

I slept on the bare cement floor on a blanket and had just one more blanket to cover me. My asthma worsened and my blood pressure problems returned. And the food was terrible. They gave us maize porridge, which was edible, but the relish was often a disgusting sauce of small rotten fish. I think they purposely made the food rot before they gave it to us. The women's officer in charge, Mrs Nyantara, was a kind woman and allowed us to do a bit of cooking for ourselves, but the men had to eat the prison food as it was served. And they were dying of dysentery in large numbers.

Fumbani

One morning shortly after our final conviction, the guards were unusually nice to me.

'Chirwa, we want you to stretch your legs today. Let's take off your chains. You can go around. Please feel free.'

I was feeling very suspicious.

'What was this now?' I thought. 'Are we going to be released or what?'

As usually they did not say anything. Things turned even stranger, when they brought a chair and urged me to sit on the veranda, and to top it all they sat a chair beside me. I faced the gate and suddenly Mr Mwale and some other high-ranking officers entered my yard. There was someone walking behind them and as they came closer I saw it was Fumbani.

They never charged Fumbani. We had not seen or heard of him since I saw him step out of the car in front of me and go into an open prison shortly after our abduction. While we were on trial for more than one and a half years, they kept Fumbani locked up and pressed him to give evidence that we had come to Malawi to kill Dr Banda. They tortured him with spanners and electrical wires and tried to turn him against his own parents. He was only 22 years old. They did not succeed in making him their crown witness. He stood against it, but Fumbani has never been the same since. He has a lot of scars on his body, but his soul is even more scarred. He gets depressed and does not want to talk to anybody. To date he does not want to tell his story and it is a big problem. I talk and talk about my suffering and it helps. If he would only open up, I think that things would clear.

He was kept in Zomba Prison close to Orton's cell, but they made an effort to keep us apart. However, one day he overheard the guards discussing our death sentence and he insisted on seeing his father. The guards might have felt pity for him and they slackened the control. A few days later he was allowed to go to the yard and do some exercises close to Orton's cell. In desperation he called out from the yard in our local language.

'Hello, big man! Are you there?'

'Fumbani? Is that you?' Orton answered from his cell.

'Yes, father, it's me!'

'Fumbani, are you okay?'

'Yes, father, I'm fine.'

'They have sentenced us to death. But don't worry, son. Some people have to die for what they believe in. Some have to die for freedom. It will be all right. Don't worry, Fumbani. You'll come out.'

Fumbani was taken back to his cell, and cried and cried.

A month later he was called to the Inspector General's office and was informed that he would be released and taken back to Zambia.

'I have to see my parents before I go,' Fumbani insisted. 'What will people say if I come back without seeing them? They might have some message or something.'

For once they were not hard on him with that and they allowed him to see us.

He sat down on the chair beside me, hugged me and cried. Tears were coming to my eyes also, but I tried to hold them back.

'If I cry now there will be chaos', I told myself and did my best to comfort him instead. 'Don't cry, Fumbani. Don't cry now. Why should you suffer like this when you have done nothing? Don't cry. It's like that. The world can be cruel, Fumbani, but don't worry. It will be all right.'

He calmed down.

'Mama, I'm about to be released and taken back to Zambia. I have come to say goodbye. I have met daddy. He sends you greetings and tells you not to worry. He is fit and just tells you to keep praying', Fumbani said.

He encouraged me and asked if there was a letter or anything else that I wanted him to take back, but I had nothing to write on and just gave him a few instructions before he left.

The secret police simply walked straight into Zambia and dropped him. There are no border posts in that area and it was very obvious to Fumbani that agents and local people alike were criss-crossing the border as they pleased. He was left on a roadside somewhere in Zambia without money, papers or anything. He fended for himself till he reached our family and friends in Lusaka and from there he went back to Dar es Salaam.

It was devastating to see Fumbani walk away like that and I was deeply worried about the future of our children. We were sentenced to death and I was certain that we were going to hang. Every time they came to pick me up it could have been for the gallows. We just had to live with that. A few months after Fumbani's visit, I was picked up one morning and taken to a room bare except for a high table covered with white linen. There was a doctor in the room and I was certain that this was the end for me.

'I am going to be slaughtered here', I thought, and started praying, 'Oh God, receive my soul.'

The doctor was especially rude to me and made an extra effort to make me feel totally distressed, as if hanging in thin air.

'Climb up!' he snarled.

The chains were taken off me and my whole body was trembling as I climbed on the table. I really saw myself as a sacrificial lamb about to be slaughtered. But it was merely a medical check-up.

Mr Mwale came to see me the following morning and I asked him what that examination was all about.

'Oh, it was just a standard medical examination. You know – to see if you are fit', he answered.

'Fit for what?'

'Fit for what? Well – just fit', he said uneasily and I knew exactly what it was all about: to see if I was fit for execution.

Orton and I had had no time together to discuss our situation and to agree on what we should do. We had a joint account and a life insurance policy, and I wanted us to ensure that our children were taken care of in case we were executed.

I asked for this meeting repeatedly, and after the medical examination I had the impression that our days were indeed numbered. I pushed harder still and finally we were allowed to meet, provided that we only discussed these practical issues.

'Vera, the children will know what to do', Orton said, but I insisted. I wanted to make sure that our assets were divided properly and that we had jointly made an effort to find the optimal arrangement for them. We had a brief talk, but the meeting was quickly broken off.

'Time's up', the guard announced. I was not to see Orton again for many, many years.

The Chains

I kept the promise I had made to Orton that last day in court and the will to live, exercise and prayers kept me going. Slowly but surely I started to build a bearable life for myself in Cell Number 2. I got permission to do a bit of digging in the courtyard and stealthily planted a few seeds I found outside my cell. The plants grew and before long the guards themselves began to give me seeds. Over the years I made a beautiful garden that supplied us all with pumpkins and beans and other vegetables. One morning the chains were also taken off.

'From now on you can walk around as you like. We have received a message from Dr Banda that you can move freely in the ward and talk to the other prisoners', the officers told me.

I was of course very pleased, but I did not connect it directly to my sentence. I knew of other prisoners with death sentences who walked around without chains, but years later some white visitors from the Red Cross informed me that Orton and I had been reprieved.

'Reprieved?' I asked.

'Yes, you were reprieved in June 1984. The death sentence was lifted and you are now serving life.'

'Oh, maybe that's why they took off my chains.'

They deliberately withheld information to torment us even further, and they even tried to chain me up again.

We were locked in our cells at 3 o'clock in the afternoon and I preferred to eat my food alone inside my cell. This day, shortly after they had removed the chains, the women's officer in charge, Mrs Nyantara, and another woman officer came to my cell after lock-up.

'How are you?' they wanted to know.

'I'm fine.'

'We are sorry, but we have received instructions to chain you again and from now on you are to be confined to this cell and not let out.'

'Why?'

'It's our instructions. We have just been told.'

'No, you're not! I'm tired of this. Please shoot me now and get it over with.'

'But, Mama, we're just carrying out our orders.'

'From whom? Go and ask why I have to be chained again and restricted to my cell. Do you realise how painful and humiliating this is? What have I done? I cooperate and follow all orders here!'

'Okay, we'll come back', they said, and went away.

I sat down to eat, but the door was thrown wide open and a male officer jumped on me. Usually a quiet man, he was now as fierce as an animal.

'Come on, chain her! Chain her!' he screamed at two young officers, who ran in after him.

They did not give me time to protest, but quickly chained my hands and feet and locked the door.

'Go to hell! You all go to hell!' I shouted at them and kneeled down in my chains to pray:

'God what is this? You freed me from the chains, but now they are back on. What have I done? I can't stand this. I can't stay chained again. Please, please God, I know you love me. Please help me!'

I prayed for about an hour, and then somebody opened the door again. It was another senior officer, two younger ones and the officer in charge of the women's ward, Mrs Nyantara.

They all entered the cell, but I did not say anything. I just stared at them.

'I'm sorry, Mrs Chirwa, there has been a mistake', the senior officer said softly. 'I can't say much, but I'm sorry. I've brought these officers here to untie you and take off the chains.'

They could see that I had cried and Mrs Nyantara tried to comfort me:

'Please, Mrs Chirwa, the chains have been removed and you have succeeded. Your prayers have been heard, now please sit down and eat some food.'

'I'm not eating anything! Why should I be treated like this? This is torture. I've done nothing wrong.'

'Now, now, God has listened to your prayers. I'm coming back in a little while and I want to see that you have eaten a bit.'

They went, and I cried as never before. It almost broke me. I threw the food in the bucket and when Mrs Nyantara came back she thought I had eaten it. I was still crying.

'It's alright, I'm here, Mrs Chirwa. Let's pray together', she said and sat beside me for a while.

When I finally fell asleep God comforted me.

I dreamed that I was flying up into the sky and Heaven opened for me. I started to come down again and I began to sing. There were people all around me – angels – and one of them said:

'Look, a human being is crying.'

I knew they were looking in my direction. I knew that I was not alone, and it filled me with joy. I was singing and as I descended all these people joined me in song. When my feet touched the ground again I was so happy:

'Thank you My Lord, because you love me. Thank you!'

God was very near to me and it kept me from being totally destroyed by the physical and mental torture I had to endure. After that revelation I always looked forward to spending my nights singing and dancing with the angels in my dreams. God saved me from going insane in there and a couple of years later I even got hold of a Bible from a prisoner who had been released. The other women prisoners quickly grabbed the clothes and utensils she had left behind, but I managed to get her Bible. I read it more than three times from Genesis to Revelation over the years.

The man who had chained me came to apologise:

'Mama, you gave us hell', he said, 'and we are very sorry, but we were following orders from Mr Mwale's deputy. It was very lucky for you that Mr Mwale was around when we went back to report. "We've done the job, sir", we told the deputy, but Mr Mwale was standing next to him and overhead the conversation.'

'What is this? What job have you ordered them to do?' he asked the deputy.

'Oh, I ordered them to chain the Chirwas', the deputy said (they had chained Orton as well). 'I received the orders from State

House, from John Tembo and from the Inspector General that we should chain and confine them again.'

'Why is it that I, the head of this prison, am not told?' Mr Mwale was furious.

'But those were the orders we received', the deputy insisted.

'No: you go and unchain them right now! The Inspector General always works through me. Whatever happens I'm in charge here! Don't forget!'

Mr Mwale sympathised with us, but his deputy was John Tembo's man and he did his best to make our lives miserable.

Torture and Maltreatment

Wanting to keep myself busy, I wrote a personal letter to Dr Banda asking for permission to write a book about Ngoni customary marriage, but I never received a reply. I soon discovered that many of the wardresses who were guarding me were illiterate. They could not even write their own names and I sent another letter and asked if I might be allowed to teach them, but there was still no response. Nevertheless, I started to teach them to write. In principle, I was not even allowed to talk to them, but I got along fine with many of them and before long they could sign their duty rosters instead of just leaving their thumbprints.

It was my luck that the water dried up in the other yard. The other women prisoners had to come to my yard, which was otherwise sealed off, to collect water. Their children were also coming and it gave me an opportunity to talk to them. I received bread, never my favourite food, as part of the prison diet, and I had asked the guards to give it to the other prisoners. It was obvious that the guards ate most of it, but as the women and children were now coming to my yard I could offer them the bread myself. I even made tea for them.

There were quite a few children in the prison. They were imprisoned with their mothers and some of them were even born inside. They were very happy to have the bread and the tea and I started to chat with them. I realised that they knew close to nothing about Jesus, and slowly but surely I started a Bible school. I told them about the Bible and I taught them to sing hymns. They gave me so much joy, these children, and they became my dearest companions in prison.

The climax of the Bible school's year arrived when Reverend Whitehouse came for Christmas. The Reverend visited the prison every year and prayed for us and brought us gifts. That year he was in for a surprise.

'Reverend, we have a choir here', I could proudly tell him and I lined up my children. They were in rags, many half-naked with their buttocks showing, but they lined up and sang four hymns.

'Ah, Chirwa!' one of the other prisoners said, 'Have you converted these ruffian children?' She was quite amazed.

They had a special place in my heart, these ragged, imprisoned children, and I did my best for them. And they helped me. When I made my garden and began to remove the concrete and the bricks from the yard, they all assisted me.

The years went by. Slowly, the restrictions were lifted and I even began to counsel the staff and the prisoners, and to interpret their dreams. However, I still had absolutely no contact with the outside world. Our second-born, Virginia, managed to get a single letter through to me, but that was all.

In the late 1980s an American woman, who had been arrested with her husband over some kind of trouble with their visa, was detained briefly in the cell next to me. To my great surprise she knew our story well. She told me that Orton and me were famous prisoners of conscience for Amnesty International, and it was indeed very comforting to learn that people all over the world were pushing for our release.

Gwanda Chakuamba, who had sided with Dr Banda during the Cabinet Crisis, had fallen from grace and was now imprisoned next to Orton. Together they smuggled out a letter about the horrible conditions and the many deaths due to the rotten food. The letter reached the International Red Cross, which sent an international delegation to Malawi to inspect the prisons in 1990.

Dr Banda was very careful about Malawi's international reputation and allowed the delegation to inspect the prisons and interview the prisoners in private. A lot of human rights violations came to light under that inspection – the awful food, the poor health and hygienic conditions, prisoners being murdered and beaten to death if they tried to escape, and so on. They interviewed me as well.

'How's my husband?' I asked them immediately, and they told me that Orton had been rather ill, but was now receiving treatment and recovering.

'Are you being tortured?' they asked me.

'No, not any more', I answered.

'No, no, you must tell us. Don't be afraid', they insisted, but I was not afraid. I held back because I pitied the women guards, whose hard-earned jobs were hanging by a thread.

Many of our guards could not read or write and a job like this was everything to them and to their children. They were going to suffer badly if they were dismissed, and they were only following the prison policy. The prison as a whole was the problem and not the behaviour of the individual guards. So, I only reported the maltreatment in general terms, mentioning the issue of the Jehovah's Witnesses.

Dr Banda had been infuriated by the Jehovah's Witnesses' effort to dissuade people from renewing their party membership and paying tax. He had publicly disowned them as 'dangerous to the good government of the state' and allowed the Young Pioneers to persecute the sect. Jehovah's Witnesses were killed and raped, their houses and shops burnt to the ground, and thousands fled from the state-sponsored violence to neighbouring Mozambique. In the prison the Jehovah's Witness prisoners were treated very badly. One day a group of them came to our ward and three women guards, who were also members of the Young Pioneers, lined them up and beat them with sticks. It was gruesome.

'What are you doing!' I yelled at them. 'You are not supposed to beat them up. They are prisoners and they are already helpless. Don't you know that it's an offence? You are going to be prosecuted!'

They stopped and I later heard that they were grumbling about me:

'Ah, this Vera Chirwa failed to take the government from Banda and now she has come here to control us.'

They feared me, which was good, because I'm sure they thought twice about molesting the prisoners when I was around.

One of the three Young Pioneer guards, Ms Chimbali, was especially cruel. A few days later, I heard crying in the ward and ran to see what was going on. Chimbali, holding a big stick, was busy humiliating the Jehovah's Witnesses again. It was a small family: a woman, her daughter and her grandchildren. Chimbali had made the two women strip and expose their private parts to the children. They were all crying, because it is strictly taboo for children to see their parents and grandparents like that. She was also beating them with her stick.

'What are you doing? You are not even supposed to be here. You're on nightshift!' I managed to get hold of her stick. 'You are not allowed to beat these women!'

'I'm going to beat them', she snapped back and started to struggle with me.

'What have they ever done to you?'

'They are Jehovah's Witnesses! They don't pay tax!' she screamed at me.

'That's not your problem!' As we struggled over the stick the officer in charge, Mrs Nyantara, rushed to the scene.

'Stop it! What is this?'

'Look, Mama', I told her, 'She's humiliating these poor women and beating them up!'

'No, Chimbali, what is all this you are doing? Shouldn't you have left long time ago? Go home!' And Chimbali angrily trotted off.

I reported incidents of this kind to the Red Cross delegation, but I left out the guards' names, and things improved dramatically after that. The guards were terrified. Many of their colleagues in other prisons and in the male section had been dismissed – some were even imprisoned – but they soon realised that I had not reported on them specifically, and we became friends.

'Oh, she's a woman of God. She has the power to forgive', they said – and they improved themselves.

Meeting Orton

It was 25 September 1992. We had spent more than ten years behind bars since our abduction on Christmas Eve in 1981. I was collected from my cell and as usual I was not told what was going to happen. I was escorted to a room in the main hall of the prison where I suddenly found myself facing a group of neatly dressed white men and women. Who were they? What was this all about?

'We are lawyers from Britain. I'm Paul Harris.' As their spokesman he introduced the five others, all barristers and solicitors from a joint Human Rights Delegation of the Scottish Faculty of Advocates, the Law Society of England and Wales, and the General Council of the Bar. When we all knew each other they brought Orton in.

We had not seen each other for more than eight years. It was such a deeply passionate moment that I cannot describe it adequately. We hugged each other for a long, long time. It was totally quiet. We did not talk, just held each other. And the lawyers sat there quietly, all of them.

'I thought you were dead', Orton finally said and looked me straight in the eyes.

'I thought you were dead too.'

'I feared it so much', he said, 'and I kept telling myself: "It's your fault. Why should you bring somebody's daughter to die in this horrible place and still be alive yourself?"'

'No, no, my dear, you shouldn't think like that. I came here on my own, because I wanted to be with you. Haven't you noticed that? It was even my own idea to go to the meeting in Chipata with you that day. Don't blame yourself. You're guilty of nothing, Orton.'

We thanked God that we had been allowed to meet. God had entered. We remembered that we were not alone and sat down with the lawyers.

They had come to make an assessment of Malawi's legal system and to build links with the Law Society of Malawi. Paul Harris told us that they had been writing to Dr Banda urging him to release us. He had not reacted and now they had come to meet him in person and intercede on our behalf. But Dr Banda had refused their request:

'I will never, never release Orton and Vera. Never!' he had told them. 'They are going to die in there.'

They had been given permission to see us and had insisted on seeing us together so that we could meet. They had wanted to see us in private without the guards, but the Inspector General had refused.

'It doesn't matter', Orton told them. 'We have nothing to hide here.'

They asked us about our health and the conditions we were living under. It was so very, very sad to hear Orton's story. I thought I had been mistreated, but he had undergone far greater

Life President Hastings Kamuzu Banda with his Mbumba
at the Independence Day celebrations, 6 July 1986

Courtesy of *The Daily Times*

hardships. He had been chained more than me, especially after
they had discovered another letter that he and Chakuamba had
tried to smuggle out. Apparently, Mrs Chakuamba had been
careless and failed to post it right after they had given it to her, and
the police had found it during a house search. They had chained
their hands and feet together after that, so that they could not lie
down but had to squat, and two guards had been set over them to
make sure they did not sleep. They had starved him and he was
constantly suffering from pneumonia and asthma in the small,

damp and badly ventilated cell. It was devastating to hear how Dr Banda had tortured the very man who had handed him his presidency. The lawyers were very moved by his story.

'Mr Chirwa, you have suffered so much', Paul Harris said, ' Can you allow us to go and ask the British Government to tell Banda to set you free? You might never be free in this country under Dr Banda's rule, but the British Government can possibly arrange that you are brought out of Malawi.'

British lawyers are very composed people, who pick their words carefully, but I think Paul Harris soon wished he had not suggested this. Orton exploded.

'Me! Running from my country! What are you talking about? Do you think I'm a coward? Do you think I can leave my people here to suffer? No, no, not me. As their leader, I will never leave them. I would rather die with them right here in prison.'

He might have been physically weak and tormented, but he was as strong in spirit as ever. He had the same spark in the eyes that I had seen in court when the police officers had mocked him and told him he would die in prison.

'I'm prepared to die', he had snapped back at them in the court-room. 'Jesus Christ died and that's why we are free today. I'm prepared to die for the Malawian people and for their freedom.'

He had kept that fighting spirit and it flared up at the lawyers' suggestion that he would give up the struggle to save his own skin.

'No, no, Orton', I interrupted. 'These people are trying to help. You can't see yourself, but you look like a man who has suffered, and they are just trying to support us. They are not con-sidering you to be a coward.'

'I'm sorry', Paul Harris said. 'We understand how you feel and we are not saying that you should run away from your people. Your story has moved us and we want to help you.'

'I'll never run away from my people', Orton continued. 'I don't care if they kill me. There is no freedom without suffering.'

In my own heart I was telling myself: 'Yah, we suffered in the British prisons and we got our freedom. And now we are suffering again in a Malawian prison.'

The lawyers now turned to the prison officers and demanded that we should receive proper treatment:

'You are not allowing them to see each other. Why can't they have visitors? And they can't write letters to their children. What kind of torture is this?'

The lawyers were quite appalled. They insisted that we should see each other, be allowed to write and receive letters, and have visitors. The prison officers had to call the Inspector General again, but they came back and promised that our rights would be respected from now on.

'We are coming back', Paul Harris said, 'and when we come we want to hear better stories about their treatment. The human rights violations in this place are unheard of!'

Orton asked if we could have a moment to ourselves. We said goodbye to the lawyers and they left the room with the prison officers.

'Let's sing', Orton said, and we sang the hymn 'We have heard Lord God that you bless other people, bless us as well'. We sang three hymns together before the warder came and interrupted us.

'Since you are going to see each other next week, you might want to sum up and say goodbye', he said.

We hugged and exchanged a few final words:

'We are going to be free, Vera.'

'Are we?'

'Yes, dear. The people of Malawi know that we, the ministers, were right. We told them that Banda was a dictator and people have realised that it was true. I'm hearing reports that Malawians have taken up arms against Banda. They want us to be free and they want me as President. Don't worry. We are going to be out very soon.'

'Oh, really, Orton? I would be so pleased to see my children again!'

'Yah, don't worry. We are getting out!'

He left the room first. We had to go down a flight of stairs to get out of the main building and into our cells, but on the stairs he turned around and insisted on seeing me again.

'You can't leave without shaking hands in our tradition', he explained to the warders, and came back up. He took my arms and prayed for me.

'Well, my dear, remember to remind them about our visits. Tell them that they have promised that we can see each other once a week. I'll remind them too, of course, but you're the activist. Don't forget to remind them.'

'I'll be reminding them', I assured him.

He went down the stairs and I never saw him alive again.

'Mr Chirwa has left us'

'When are you going to organise that meeting', I asked the officer in charge.

'I've been calling the Inspector General, but he hasn't authorised it yet. He has to give permission and he has to get his permission from State House.'

The first week passed. The second week after the lawyers' visit I reminded them three times, but they kept telling me that permission had not yet been granted.

'Why? Banda and the Inspector General have already agreed to this. They agreed and you told the white lawyers that we were going to meet once a week.'

'I don't know what's happening', the prison officer said.

One morning exactly four weeks after the visit I heard a lot of commotion from the men's section. In fact, Orton and I had been separated only by a high wall for the last eleven years and you could easily hear that something was going on over there. The guards told me that the men had their six-monthly 'meat day' and were fighting to get as much as possible, but why would they fight over the food so early in the morning? I tried to eat my breakfast, but I was disturbed by this incident and had lost my appetite. I sat down on my veranda, my back against the cell door and my legs stretched out, and began to read the Bible.

At 11 o'clock a group of people entered my yard. First, I saw the senior women prisoners from the other blocks, then the prison officers, then some police officers.

'What is this?' I thought, 'What have I done now?'

It was unusual that the other women prisoners had come, and I was quite confused. Every time Mr Mwale came to my cell he always greeted me and asked how I was doing, but that day he did not say a word. His face was drawn. They all came up to the veranda and the women sat down next to me.

'So, what's the problem?' I asked

Mr Mwale cleared his throat: 'I'm sorry, Mrs Chirwa. Mr Chirwa has left us.'

My head was spinning: 'Left us? Has he gone to another prison? No, that can't be since this is the central prison. . . . Has he been released?'

I was thinking hard and Mr Mwale saw that he had me confused.

'He died this morning. He was found dead in his cell.'

I just looked back at them. Nobody said a word for some very long moments.

'Banda must be very happy now that my husband is dead', I finally told them. 'He has killed him.'

'Well, Mrs Chirwa, it is indeed mysterious. You know that I always go to see him after everybody else is locked up and I went there yesterday and chatted, and he was all right. So this morning I was very surprised to hear that that he was found dead,' Mr

Mwale said, 'But I can assure you, Mrs Chirwa, that we are going to investigate this. We are very sorry.'

'My God! Orton! My life is finished!' I cried.

The officers left and the women tried to comfort me.

'Don't touch me! I don't want to be touched. Leave me alone', I told them.

It seemed that a terrible cloud had fallen on me. I could not imagine my life without Orton. I loved him so much and he cared for me. The father of my children, who taught me everything and encouraged me to become a politician, was dead. I started to talk like a mad woman.

'No, no! It can't be true!'

'Oh, Mama, please. . .' the women comforted me, but I wanted them to go away.

'Don't touch me! Don't talk to me!'

I thought about the children hearing of their father's death and I cried and cried. It was the worst moment of my life, and I started to pray.

Mr Mwale came back.

'You women are not going to sleep in your own cells tonight. From now on you stay here and look after Mrs Chirwa day and night. I don't want anything to happen to her like what happened to her husband!'

Mr Mwale was fed up with it all. He was a good man.

The true story of Orton's death remains to be told. Orton had a young boy cooking for him. Orton taught him to become a good Christian and used to counsel him and sing with him. This cook had a friend, who was caught with some heroin in the prison and put in disciplinary isolation right opposite Orton's cell. The night Orton died this boy heard footsteps outside the cells. He thought they were coming to teach him a lesson and he pulled himself up and peeped out of the bars above the cell door. He saw a group of people, including the medical assistant of the prison, a minister in Dr Banda's government, a high-ranking police officer and some other police officers. The medical assistant was carrying something, which was covered with a piece of cloth. They went to Orton's cell for a while and the boy saw them all leave again. They had given Orton a lethal injection.

When I later founded Malawi CARER, the rights-awareness NGO, the British lawyer Kathryn English and I took corroborative statements from a number of prisoners and staff who had been around that night. They approached us to tell their story, but they were very nervous and all of them later disappeared.

Mr Mwale came back the next morning.

'Mrs Chirwa, I don't want Orton to be buried like a dog, like they bury people here without the relatives knowing. So, whom shall I contact? Who are the closest relatives?'

It was hard for me to guide him, because we had had absolute no contact with our relatives for 11 years.

'My uncle Mackinley Chiwambo has a son, Ziriro. Maybe you can contact him', I said.

'I know him. He's my friend. Let me call him and make sure that he can make the proper arrangements so that Orton gets a decent burial.'

The International Red Cross came in the afternoon and offered their condolences and their help. I was certain that the government wanted to kill our children and I asked the Red Cross to find out how they could safely attend the funeral. I also asked them to plead with the government that I could be present as well, and they promised to try their best.

Mr Mwale had worked very quickly and I was called to the gate that very evening. I saw a woman and three men sitting outside waiting for me.

'These are your relatives', Mr Mwale said.

The woman was my younger sister Chris, whom I had not seen

in all these years. The other men were my nephews.

'We have come to find out where you want Mr Chirwa to be buried so we can make the proper arrangements.'

'Ah, it's very difficult for me, because according to our tradition it's our first-born, Fumbani, and Orton's brother, Duff Chirwa, who should decide. But since they are not here I request that Mr Chirwa be buried at home in his village.'

'Okay', they said.

'I have also received a telegram from a lady in America,' Mr Mwale added. ' She says she's Mr Chirwa's first-born, and that she is also coming.'

'That's good', I said. 'She's his daughter from his first marriage. When she comes she can decide everything, but until then you can go ahead with the arrangements.'

My sister was crying her heart out and telling me that I looked terrible. She was very sad to see me like this.

They went and Mr Mwale promised that I could see Orton's body after the post mortem.

I waited to see the body. After five days I thought they had just gone ahead and buried him, but late in the evening the women guards came to my cell.

'Come on, we are going to the gate.'

'To the gate? Why are you bothering me now? What are we going to do at the gate at this time?'

'We don't know, but the officers have called and you are wanted at the gate.'

They escorted me to the gate and took me outside, where a lot of police cars were waiting. I got into one of them and we drove off.

After 12 years in prison I did not recognise Zomba town again. There were lights all over and I did not know where they were taking me. We drove through a huge gate and there were police guards everywhere. We stopped in front of a large building and the police officers were running around. We entered the building and I recognised the smell of a mortuary.

'Can it be that I'm going to see Orton's body after all?', I wondered, but I could not ask anybody. They were all silent. They put me on a chair between two policewomen. We waited. I wondered if they wanted to kill me as well.

'If this is death for me as well, let me start praying', I told myself and I prayed. 'Please God, give me courage, if I'm to see Orton's body. Please be with me.'

An hour later somebody called:

'Okay, take her there', and we walked and walked through long dark corridors, crossed a courtyard and came to a large room.

There were quite a number of plain-clothes men and women in the room. They had lined up on either side of an ambulance with its back doors open, backed up against an open door at the other end. Everybody was completely mute. I got into the ambulance. He was lying on a stretcher there, not in a coffin, and I immediately recognised his legs. It was my husband.

'Come, come, come', they signalled to me, and I went all the way in and stood right beside his head. All the police officers were very quiet. And I prayed.

I expressed everything in my prayer. We had promised to be together till death and that day death parted us. I prayed for an hour. I wanted to touch him, but the police officers got nervous and ran to ask for permission.

'Yes, you can touch him', they finally said and I touched him.

'Goodbye my dear, we'll meet, when I also die. Amen.' I turned to the long line of police officers. 'I have finished.'

They drove me back to my cell.

Kissing the Ground

The children came to Malawi under heavy security and were taken straight from the airport to the American Embassy. They took their father's body to his village up north and buried him. A few days later I had visitors.

The guards took me to a dark room in the prison building. The sun had just set and my eyes were not well: the necessary medical treatment had not been provided in the prison. There were some people in the room, but I could not see them properly. I sat down and they all rushed to hug me. The girls started crying.

'Oh, these are my children', I realised.

My cousins, nephews and nieces were also there and I recognised all of them – except one, who had grown completely out of recognition and was wearing a beard. I looked at him for some time.

'Who is this gentleman?' I asked, and it came out rather funny, because I used a very formal way of speech in our local language, addressing him as an important man.

He got up and hugged me hard.

'I'm Zengani, Mama', he said and I was so ashamed.

'Ai, ai, ai! How long have I been in this prison if I can't even recognise my own child! I'm sorry, Zengani, but you have grown so much.'

We all dropped tears. It was a beautiful moment.

They told me about the funeral.

'Mama, we don't think that the body they gave us was our father.'

'Why?'

'No, the body they showed us was so very black. We said it couldn't be our father.'

I was shocked. When I saw Orton's body he was very peaceful and relaxed and he looked almost like a young man.

'But I saw him myself, and I'm sure it was your father', I assured them.

'We don't know, Mama. First, we refused to accept the body. It was so black. We don't know. . . .'

We discussed this for some time; later, I discovered that this extreme blackening of the corpse is likely to have been an effect of a particular kind of lethal injection. After some time the body goes totally black.

'You are not treating our mother well!' The children were attacking the prison officers who were guarding the door. 'Why can't she see? Are you beating her eyes?'

'No, I can see', I comforted them.

'No, we can see that you are not well, Mama.'

'Look, I'm quite all right. Don't leave here thinking that I'm ill or about to die or something. I'm okay. Don't worry.'

They showed me an album with family photos and I had trouble seeing the pictures properly and mistook photos of my granddaughters for my own daughters. They all resembled me very much, and it was wonderful to see them. I was allowed to take the photos to my cell and we said goodbye.

A few days later they drove me back to the building where I had seen Orton's body. I realised that it was Police Headquarters. I was taken to an office arranged around a huge desk with telephones everywhere. There must have been six telephones on that desk. A man entered and busily answered a lot of calls. Eventually he turned towards me and presented himself as the Inspector General. He told me that he was very sorry about Orton's death and that he would have come to see me, but had been far too busy.

'I'm not happy with you!' I'm not a person who keeps things in the heart and I told him this straight to his face.

'Why?' He was a bit shocked.

'You did a very bad thing. When the lawyers were here you promised that my husband and I could see each other once a week.

But it never happened. The prison officers said they needed your permission and that you needed approval from State House. Why? It had been agreed on that day and the permission granted. Three weeks later I hear that my husband is dead, and we never had a chance to sit down together. That's why I'm not happy with you!'

He was quiet for some time, looking down and evading my eyes.

'I'm sorry. It's not my fault', he said. 'It's true that the permission was given that day and I see no reason why the prison officers failed to let you see each other.'

'No, no, no! I trust the officer in charge of the prison. He is telling the truth. This thing lies with you!'

'Anyway, I'm sorry', he said, and started to make excuses. He accused senior politicians of pressurising him and trying to make themselves popular by prolonging our misery. I listened him out, and we started to talk about my future.

'I want to see the children and I want to receive letters from them and from my relatives.'

'I'll personally call your relatives and make sure they come and visit you', he said. 'I like you, Mama. I also pray very much. I have asked Banda about your release twice already, but he just sends me away. I'll ask again. So, pray for me.'

'Okay, I'll pray for you', I said and off he went.

The following week I was called to the gate again.

'Ah, all this coming and going', I complained to the guards. 'You are just bothering me. Leave me alone or release me.'

'No, no, you have to go. We don't know what the message is', the woman guard said.

I was taken back to the Inspector General's office.

'Mama, you wanted to see your relatives so I invited Ziriro Chiwambo, but he is busy campaigning for multi-party democracy. His brother, Rodney, is coming to see you instead', the Inspector General said.

A message was delivered that my visitor had come and the Inspector General asked him to enter the office, but my sister and my cousins came along as well.

'What is this? I only invited Rodney Chiwambo', the Inspector General asked.

'We Chiwambos have agreed that if one of us is called we will all go', they told him, 'So many people are being arrested these days and if one of us disappears we don't know what has happened. Therefore we all go together.'

'Oh, I see', the Inspector General laughed. 'Anyway, let me break the news then. I did not want you to hear this in prison and brought you here. From today Mrs Chirwa is free.'

They all got very confused – except me. I just watched him intently. My sister fell to the ground and praised the Lord.

'Oh God, thank you very much. Thank you, thank you.'

I waited for all of them to recover from the shock.

'On what conditions are you releasing me?'

'What do you mean', he asked.

'Some people are released under certain restrictions – house arrest, expulsion, or whatever. What are the conditions?'

'Oh, no, no. There are no restrictions. You are very released. You can do what you like!'

We left his office as very, very happy people and they dismissed my guard.

'You can go now. Mrs Chirwa is free.'

I wanted to go back to the prison. I had to say goodbye to my fellow prisoners, but it was after 3 o'clock and they were all locked inside their cells. They called the officer in charge.

'Mrs Chirwa is free, but she wants to say goodbye. Please make sure that the women prisoners are out of their cells.'

We went back to the women's ward and they were already out on the veranda singing hymns. I joined them and said goodbye to each and every one. It was very moving. I went to my cell and picked up the few belongings that were mine.

I had always told myself that if I was released and was to see the outside world again I would kiss the earth. When we went out, after saying goodbye to all the prisoners and the officers, I stooped and kissed the ground right outside the prison gates. My sister broke down in tears.

'Tell me now that these are tears of happiness', I said, and hugged her.

It was 24 January 1993. I was free.

8 Back in Civil Society

I could not sleep in a bed. I was staying with my sister, Chris, and we were sleeping side by side the first night after my release, but I felt seasick and dizzy moving around on the soft mattress. After some time I had to climb down and lie on the floor, where I was used to sleeping. Chris woke up.

'What on earth are you doing on the floor, Vera?'

'I can't sleep in a bed anymore, Chris', I explained, 'I feel like falling down all the time.'

She cried. It really got to her, I think, to see her older sister lying on the floor like a prisoner. I tried to rest in the bed to comfort her, but when she fell asleep, I gingerly came down to the floor. I slept like that for several weeks till I got used to beds again, always hurrying back to bed when I heard Chris move in her sleep.

My life in prison had been dedicated to prayer and I had worried whether I would be able to continue to pray after my release. It might be hard to understand, but I genuinely feared that I would lose the spiritual life, which had kept me alive inside the prison. Would I still be able to dance with the angels at night or had life on the outside become too hectic and mundane? Thus, it was very comforting to receive my first visitors in Chris's house. They all came in a spirit of joy and prayer. We prayed and sang hymns together and I found that Chris really loved praying too. When I went to church for the first time in all those years, they told me that the congregation had prayed for me the previous Sunday. When I later travelled to meet my children and family in

Zambia, Tanzania, America and Scotland, I visited their congregations and found that they had prayed for my release on that particular Sunday as well. Everywhere I went people approached me and said:

'We are so happy that our prayers for your release were answered by God.' It was very powerful.

Time for Democracy?

The American Ambassador came to visit and told me that many embassies and heads of state had pushed for my release. The American Vice-President, Al Gore, had personally written to Dr Banda, as had Kenya's President Moi, the British Queen and others. The Berlin Wall had fallen and Dr Banda could no longer play the anti-communist card and continue to uphold his ruthless regime with international funding. The international community had finally had it with his dictatorship and donors had begun to condition development aid on human rights and governance improvements. These conditionalities and sanctions had been directly linked to my release. The Ambassador also told me how Amnesty International had campaigned tirelessly for our release and that letters from Amnesty members had swamped Dr Banda for years. It was very moving to learn that so many people from all over the world had made an effort for us and had worked so hard for human rights and justice. Amnesty International even offered me a round trip to visit my family and children, who were scattered all over the world from Zambia to Canada.

I attended a lot of Amnesty International meetings and seminars on that trip and while I was addressing a student meeting in Orlando the director of Amnesty International handed me a telegram from the Malawian Law Society. They offered me a job as director of the Law Society's human rights NGO, The Legal

Vera Chirwa shortly after her release in the mid-1990s

Courtesy of *The Nation* newspaper.

Resource Centre. Dr Banda's regime was falling, but he was still in power and he could still hurt me if I returned to Malawi. Amnesty International worried about my safety. They advised me not to accept the post with the Legal Resource Centre and the director told me that they had arranged a job for me with an international agency in Geneva. But I had been away from my country for almost 30 years, exiled and imprisoned and nothing was going to keep me out of Malawi again. I had a calling to teach Malawians about their rights. The fight for justice had guided my whole life, and in prison I had promised myself that if I ever got out I would dedicate my life to the people of Malawi. How could I take a fancy job in Geneva? And I felt protected by the international community and all the good people who had fought for my release. I did not think that Dr Banda would dare to touch me again.

However, the situation was tense in Malawi. During the last few years of our imprisonment dissident groups had started to form in opposition to Dr Banda's regime. The two most prominent groups, the Alliance for Democracy (AFORD) and the United Democratic Front (UDF), worked underground and distributed 'seditious' literature that urged Malawians to stand up against the MCP government and demand multi-party democracy.

On Sunday 8 March 1992 the opposition had taken a dramatic turn. The Catholic Bishops circulated a pastoral letter called 'Living Our Faith': 16,000 copies were printed and the letter was read out in all the Catholic parishes in the country. It openly criticised the bad governance of the MCP and exposed the deep social, economic and political problems of the country. This courageous move by the bishops was a hitherto unheard-of challenge to Dr Banda's autocracy and it was soon revealed that senior MCP officials schemed to have them murdered. But people were fully behind the bishops and finally rose against the MCP. Workers and students demonstrated and many were shot dead by the police. An avalanche had been set in motion and AFORD and the UDF emerged into the open. The Churches, the Muslim community, the Law Society and the pressure groups jointly formed an umbrella organisation, the Public Affairs Committee (PAC), which started to negotiate the inevitable transition with the MCP government. On 18 October 1992, Dr Banda announced that the country would hold a referendum to determine whether Malawians wanted MCP one-party rule to continue or to introduce multi-party politics. My dear Orton sensed the end of Banda's rule only weeks before he died. Orton was murdered during the night of 19 October, immediately after Dr Banda's decision to risk a referendum.

When I returned from my round trip, the nation was holding its breath in the lead-up to the referendum for multi-party democracy in June 1993. There was violence in the streets and my family feared that I might be killed if I moved around in public. I was weak and my family urged me to stay in the house, but I longed to go out and see what was happening.

I felt strange after all those years in prison and wondered whether Malawians were actually capable of changing the government through a referendum. Malawians are a bit docile and I feared that years of oppression had pulled out their teeth completely and undercut their resolve. The all-pervading fear had crept into the souls of the people and had intimidated each and every one. In prison I had often felt that they had forgotten us. Would they finally stand up for their rights? I followed the developments on the radio and slowly began to believe.

'This is the time to get rid of Banda. This is the time for true democracy in Malawi', I thought.

But then I realised how divided the opposition was. The pressure groups were not fully united. The leaders from UDF and AFORD both came to me and asked me to join them, but I refused.

'Multi-party democracy in this country has to limit itself to two strong political organisations for a start – the government and the opposition', I told them. 'All this mushrooming of pressure groups and simmering rivalry will split the vote. We may lose the referendum if you divide yourselves. I will not join either of you!'

'No, no', they insisted. 'We are real multi-party democrats. We will form a coalition government.'

'Don't underestimate Kamuzu', I warned them. 'He has sat for a long, long time and he is well-rooted in the villages. This is not a walkover. You risk our future with this attitude.'

And of course their victory was far from total. More than a third of the voters wanted to remain under the dictator's rule.

The Chairman of the Law Society approached me shortly after I returned from my round trip.

'So, Mrs Chirwa, did you receive our offer? It's not much, but it's the only thing we can do to contribute. What do you think?'

I had had a serious discussion with my relatives, who were strongly against the idea.

'The Law Society just wants to use you. Every single lawyer in this country has turned down their offer. There's no salary. And there's no car! A director is supposed to have a car and certain amenities.'

I explained how I had prayed to be allowed to teach Malawians about their rights and this human rights NGO might be what God had in mind for me. They sympathised with that and let me have my way. I took the job and became the director of the Legal Resource Centre. They took me to the office.

'This is your secretary, Ivy Chipofya', they said, and introduced us. 'And this is your office.'

'Where are the other people?' I asked as I looked around the small, empty rooms. 'Am I going to direct myself?'

'Oh, we are sorry, but we actually hope that you will develop this for us, Mrs Chirwa', they said.

'Okay, I will' – and Ivy and I got started.

The Constitution: Reflecting the Will of the People

Our first project was to address the apparent lack of cooperation between lawyers and politicians. Constructive exchange between these two groups is a basic prerequisite for good governance and we set up a seminar where prominent members of the justice system and our new legislators could interact and find common ground.

The seminar went very well and during the final session the issue of our new Constitution came up. The chairman of the Law Society told us that a draft Constitution was just about to be finalised.

'Will the people get a chance to comment on the Constitution, as they did in South Africa?' I asked.

'No, I'm afraid not. The government has already set a date for the referendum', he said.

'Now look, it just won't do if the new Constitution is imposed on people like the old one. The people will never fully own it if they don't get a chance to participate. Let's organise a Constitutional Symposium, where as many people as possible can discuss it with invited experts from other Commonwealth countries. We need an opportunity to sit down and discuss our new Constitution, before we are asked to accept it.'

We agreed to set up a symposium and invited a group of international experts on constitutional law. The Malawian delegates were an extensive mix of representatives from interest groups, community organisations, professional associations, traditional communities and so on. It was a very big event and I was on the radio a lot informing and encouraging people to participate. And Dr Banda did not oppose it.

Ivy and I worked round the clock and financed many of our expenses out of our own pockets. It was thus quite disappointing, when the chairman of the Law Society started to make demands about certain formalities regarding the papers we were supposed to forward to the keynote speakers. We had absolutely no administrative back-up or funds and decided to hand out the agenda and relevant papers to the symposium participants as they arrived. But the chairman insisted that all papers should be forwarded in advance and challenged me – either I cancelled the symposium or he refused to attend. I knew that I was doing the right thing, and if I am doing the right thing, nobody can stop me.

'I'm not going to attend', he threatened on the phone.

'I'm sorry, but I'm going ahead with this, Mr Chairman. People have already started to come. Tickets and accommodation are booked. We can't cancel now.'

He slammed the phone down. I called Ivy and told her what had happened. We had worked hard for this and she was just as tough as I am.

'We can't cancel now, Mama. We have to go ahead.'

We had invited an expert on land rights, Mr Johnny Becker, who was quite alarmed when he heard that Ivy and I were struggling with this symposium on our own. He immediately offered to find us some assistance and sent us the CVs of a British couple, Kathryn English and Adam Stapleton, who were both lawyers. We managed to get some funding for their airfares to Malawi and they came to our assistance as volunteers. It was a great help. Kathryn immediately took charge of the secretariat.

There was a lot of excitement about the symposium. Every village headman wanted to come and registrations kept pouring in. Even Kadzamira wanted to come. She was still Dr Banda's official hostess. Down the years her family, and in particular her uncle John Tembo, had won considerable influence over the leader. As the Life President's health was deteriorating they were to an increasing extent running the country, and the former nurse of our erstwhile family doctor had become a very powerful woman indeed. I suppose she was curious to know what this symposium was all about.

We began to communicate through our sisters. Kadzamira sent her sister to see my sister and indicated that she might want to attend. Chris came and asked me:

'Kadzamira's sister visited me and it seems Kadzamira wants to know if she can attend the symposium.'

'Of course she can attend. It's not a matter of who she is or isn't. She's a citizen of Malawi and she can attend.'

The message reached Kadzamira and she decided to phone me directly. However, our new friend Kathryn had landed the day before and she answered the phone.

'Who are you?' Kathryn wanted to know.

Kadzamira became nervous on hearing an unfamiliar foreigner's voice, and kept quiet.

'Who are you? If you can't tell me your name, you can't talk to Vera Chirwa. You must tell me who you are and why you want to speak to her.'

I overheard the conversation and it suddenly struck me: 'Maybe it is Kadzamira.'

'Let me have the phone, Kathryn', I said. 'Hello, who are you?'

'It's me, Mama.' I immediately recognised Kadzamira's voice. 'I want to attend the symposium.'

Ah-ah, Kadzamira was serious about this after all, I thought and said: 'You are free to attend it. You can come, but where do we put you? You will have to choose where you want to sit.'

'No, it doesn't matter. I'll just sit anywhere.'

'Don't fool us! You are big people, and we have to give you due respect. You can't just sit with anyone. I know that. Please tell me where to put you.'

'Okay, you can put us with the diplomats', she said.

The symposium was opened and it went very well. I had made a special effort to put women in trusted posts as chairs of the sessions, conveners, and facilitators. The Law Society was formally the organiser, but its chairman still insisted on his boycott. The secretary showed up and he was visibly pleased to receive a bit of credit for the Society when I urged him to come forward from the audience and answer a particular question.

I gave a little speech about our imprisonment and about the kangaroo court we had been dragged through. We discussed local and traditional courts and I could of course testify vividly to the incompetence of the chiefs and their appalling statements – like the time when Chief Nazombe, who presided over our case, had said:

'We are here to deal with people like you. The owner of this court has put us here to convict all those who are against him!'

Quite a few people got uneasy and I suddenly remembered that Kadzamira was among the participants. I had been busy with some foreign lawyers when she had arrived and had not had the chance to greet her. But my speech was not directed at her. I was just recalling what we had been through.

After the session she walked up to the platform and shook hands with me.

'This is wonderful', she said. 'We need people like you – women who are brave.'

'Thank you very much', I said, and off she went. I was very happy for that.

It was the first time in the Banda era that Malawians had participated in such a debate – open, practical and principled – about governance and polity. Even the President himself was acknowledging our work and endorsing the symposium.

'It's very good what Mrs Chirwa is doing', he said on the radio. 'I want this sort of thing to happen in Malawi. I want things to go well constitutionally in our country.'

People were shocked. They all thought that the leader wanted to kill me or put me back in prison at the first opportunity.

'You don't know Kamuzu Banda', I told them. 'When it comes to matters of principle he can sometimes support you, if he thinks that it's the right thing to do.'

The decisions and recommendations from the symposium formed the basis of the new Constitution. A subsequent confer-ence was held some time later, where I presented a paper on how the Commission of Inquiry, the Office of the Ombudsman and the National Compensation Tribunal could advance democracy and human rights protection in Malawi.

It was a dream coming true for me to bring my professional skills as the first woman lawyer in Southern Africa to bear on my own country. In a broad sense this was what we had been fighting for: the ushering in of a multi-party system and the ratification of the Constitution as an essential and guiding instrument in a democracy.

But the fight was far from over.

9 *Human Rights at the Fingertips*

Women's Rights

Emancipating the women of Malawi has been a basic pulse in my fight against oppression and injustice. Women need to be empowered. It is fundamental. They need to claim, defend, promote and protect their own rights and the very first step is sensitisation and awareness raising. The Constitution, by necessity, was written in a hurry and we now faced a tremendous task of bringing it to the people.

In 1993, I convened a meeting through an organisation in Blantyre that worked to encourage women to set up small businesses. The executive director was very supportive and invited me to speak to the members. The room was packed with women and I introduced my idea of establishing an NGO to promote and protect women's rights. The idea was very welcome and we started out by choosing a name. We did everything democratically. Various names were suggested, but we finally settled on Women's Voice and I was elected president.

Our primary objective was to teach women about their rights through awareness raising, civic education programmes and promotion of women's education. We wanted to be a watchdog for women in the justice system, but as the name indicated, we also wanted our organisation to be a place for debate and discussion among women and on women's issues – a forum where women's voices could be heard.

150

The issue of rape is a good example. Although the equal rights of men and women are formally secured in our Constitution, in Malawi a man is very seldom convicted of rape. It was exactly the same in Tanzania when I worked there. Women are often blamed or pressed to forgive and the whole issue of tradition seeps into the court rulings. I do not subscribe to the idea that tradition and custom *per se* are oppressive to women. Traditions are complex and can be very diverse. In Malawi we have both matrilineal and patrilineal communities, and in the matrilineal communities, where inheritance follows the woman's bloodline, women are to a greater extent in charge. Their uncles and brothers can easily chase a useless husband away after he has built nice houses and produced children. Thus, some traditions protect women, but we need to get rid of the bad ones – like the traditions of male dominance implicitly invoked in most rape cases.

Adultery cases are similarly prejudiced against women, especially in patrilineal communities. A wronged woman is always pressurised to forgive. Nobody frowns on a man who takes a lover. This acceptance is due to our tradition of polygamy, but a loose relationship without proper customary marriage obligations is not polygamy. It is sex outside a lawful marriage, which even the chiefs in the local courts, who are supposed to preside over these cases, forget. However, when a woman has an extramarital affair, there is no talk of forgiveness and the man often breaks the marriage ruthlessly, with the blessing of the traditional courts. Women's voices need to be heard.

I was still director of the Legal Resource Centre when we formed Women's Voice. Kathryn and Adam helped out, but Ivy and I were the only staff. The Resource Centre was a human rights NGO, with a mandate that obviously included women's rights, but when women started to come to us with their problems the chairman got upset.

'This is not a women's organisation', he complained.

'Oh, but I thought a human rights organisation was open to all – including women', I replied. Despite this he made me agree to downplay women's rights issues in the organisation. The Law Society's leadership, it seemed, was jealous of the success of the symposium and the interest it had generated in my work, and shortly after our discussion on the women's issue they called me in for a meeting.

'We hear that you present yourself as the owner and founder of the Resource Centre, when you are approached by journalists', the chairman barked at me.

'What do you mean?'

'Yes, you think you are clever,' said the secretary general, quite a young man, 'but we know what you're up to.'

'Who has told you these lies? Tell me and we can sort this out.' But they were very aggressive and continued to call me names, ridiculing me for being an old, useless woman.

I went home. I missed Orton terribly and cried all night. How could these young people demean me like this out of petty jealousy after all the hard work Ivy and I had put into the Resource Centre? It had become a success thanks to us, but from now on they could have it for themselves. I resigned.

In prison I had dreamed of forming two organisations – one with a special focus on women and one with a broader focus on human rights and the administration of justice in general. After Women's Voice it was time to take the second step. Ivy quickly quit the Resource Centre as well. We teamed up with a bright young lawyer and jointly formed Malawi CARER: the Malawi Centre for Advice, Research and Education on Rights. We received invaluable support from Professor Gillings and his wife Jennifer, who helped us find office premises, and we soon got our first bit of funding from the UNDP.

CARER was one of the first NGOs of its kind in Malawi and is today among the country's leading human rights organisations. We formulated a twofold commitment for the new organisation: to combat the ignorance that enabled our human rights to be violated so easily for more than 30 years of dictatorship, and to contribute to making justice accessible to the country's marginalised groups.

In Malawi CARER we have always based our activities on the grassroots and our first programme, quite tellingly, was an assessment of actual human rights needs in the rural areas. What did most Malawians know about human rights? What role could human rights play in their lives? What initiatives would make a difference and be welcomed by the people? We set up a huge survey and sent people to interview women, youth, chiefs and other significant groups about their knowledge of human rights.

We learned that chiefs had conspicuously little knowledge of human rights despite their capacity as village headmen and their decisive roles in local disputes, and we decided to launch a sensitisation programme for them. A cornerstone of Malawi CARER's work is the paralegals, and it is safe to say that we were champions of paralegals in Malawi. Despite the reform of the justice sector many people in rural areas feel completely alienated from the legal system. Legal services are expensive and rural communities seldom have access to lawyers. Paralegals play a valuable role in this respect. They are lay people who obtain a basic legal training on the basis of which they offer a free advice-and-referral service to their communities. In that way they empower the communities by making rural people understand and participate in the delivery of justice. Paralegals can function as legal advisers, conflict solvers and, not least, trainers. We started to educate paralegals whom we sent into the field as human rights operatives. It worked fantastically well and we had a positive response from the chiefs.

'Why have you not come earlier?' they often asked. 'Things have changed so dramatically in politics and we know nothing about it.

You people mainly criticise us for being undemocratic, but we don't know about democracy!'

The training was well received and it expanded to the lay magistrates as well. When these lower and traditional courts are trying a case they are now able to balance the proceedings on the basis of human rights. However, the assessment also made it clear that we needed a continuous presence in the districts to sustain the work and we began to establish district offices for the paralegals throughout the country. Today, Malawi CARER is able to train 20 paralegal officers a year and the organisation has no fewer than nine district offices. Such an extensive and ambitious organisation needs considerable funding, of course, and it is always a challenging task to secure funds from donors, but we have managed well so far. American and Dutch donors have supported us generously, but we have also suffered from policy changes or sudden new requirements from our donors, which in some cases have disrupted our activities.

A more devastating disruption of our activities was the loss of Ivy. When we started Malawi CARER, I accidentally ran into the head of the Swedish development agency, SIDA, on a trip to Europe, and I asked her for a bit of funding. She was quite fed up with supporting Malawians who did not deliver, but she said that, since I was a woman, she would take one more chance. She gave us a grant and Ivy and I went on a research trip to other Southern African countries to learn from their paralegal programmes. The Legal Resources Foundation in Zimbabwe became our role model and Ivy undertook full training there as a paralegal. She came back to lead the paralegal section of Malawi CARER and Ivy, Kathryn English and I worked together as a formidable team.

Ivy was the backbone of the establishment of paralegalism in Malawi CARER, a development which later led to many other organisations taking up paralegalism. Unfortunately she passed away in 2003.

At the Grassroots

During the constitutional process I made a special effort to involve and promote as many women speakers as possible. All the male decision makers knew me well, but they were shocked to see that I was far from being the only woman who could stand up and present a political argument with insight and force. Together we were drawing attention to women's issues – domestic violence, property grabbing, inheritance, reproductive health – and we fought hard to establish a second chamber, a Senate. We backed the idea of a Senate that would have a special quota for women and thus balance the obvious under-representation of women in Parliament, but in the end this provision was dropped and the Constitution amended. While it was argued that a Senate was too costly to run, this outcome obviously reflected the interests of the new government and marked the beginning of a dark series of constitutional amendments in which the government tried to refashion our hard-earned constitutional democracy to serve its own interests.

In a nascent democracy like ours it is so very important to bring the Constitution to the people and give them an opportunity to understand its significance. Without that kind of public ownership the sitting government meets little broad-based resistance when it tries to undermine the Constitution by amending it. The human rights organisations have joined hands to bring the Constitution to the people by simplifying it and translating it into the main local languages, but copies run out very quickly and we need more funds. Malawi CARER has made and distributed a short, simple booklet on Chapter Four of the Constitution, which concerns human rights, but dissemination of information needs to go hand in hand with training and sensitisation. Human rights NGOs have to take on that responsibility and it is a tremendous task – especially where women are concerned.

Rural women are so ignorant of their rights. Some women even believe that their husbands do not love them properly if they are not beaten regularly, and this ignorance makes them vulnerable. They accept the continuous violation of their rights as a way of life, and it is hard to change their mindset and get the potentially very transformative idea of human rights across to them.

In Malawi CARER and Women's Voice we use drama and poetry to address the problem of property grabbing. The term refers to the widespread practice of unlawfully disinheriting widows. The deceased husband's relatives grab the land and chase the woman and her children away, so that they end up in extreme hopelessness with no way of sustaining themselves. And it is explained away as a tradition! Even Dr Banda tried to change this tradition and passed a law that assured women's right to inherit, but people rejected it.

'In our culture, women can't inherit,' the tribal elders argued, and property grabbing continued.

It is important to recognise that the colonial government and Dr Banda were equally wrong in approaching this problem by *imposing* laws on the people. It is even more frustrating that our democratically elected government now continues this top-down legislation, which obviously does not work on its own. The legal basis for change has improved considerably with the Wills and Inheritance Act, but it needs to be introduced properly to the people. The parliamentarians should encourage their constituencies to discuss it and ultimately embrace it, but they fail to involve their own voters.

I have experienced a similar unwillingness to allow people to participate voiced by quite a different camp. An American women activist visited Malawi and encouraged the women's organisation to press for a bill against domestic violence, an idea which had been adopted in other countries.

'It's a fine idea', I got up and said, 'but we as women repre-sentatives should not just agree to have this bill. Let's go and introduce it to the men and women in rural and urban areas. Let them have their say, because I'm sure there will be a lot of resistance to it. We can only start to campaign for the bill after such a debate.'

'Oh, no', the American woman said. 'Laws are made by a few people to make everybody else obey. This is how you transform a society!' And all the others, lawyers and activists alike, supported her.

In Malawi CARER and Women's Voice we strive to take a different approach. We invite people to gather in the villages for a meeting, including the chiefs and elders, and paralegals and community educators from our NGOs engage in a dialogue with women and men to show that this practice is wrong and that victimised women can get redress. Women's Voice have trained women paralegals, who originate from the rural communities and know the culture of the people. They are formally uneducated women, but they manage to keep the contents and principles of Chapter Four of the Constitution in their heads. African women are supposed to be shy and people are very surprised when one of our paralegals, a woman from their own community, courageously stands up and speaks before the whole village. I am very proud of them.

The paralegal explains the law, tells about women's and children's rights and announces that a play will be performed, and that everyone will be able to discuss it afterwards. The play presents and illuminates a property-grabbing case: many facets are brought out.

A couple get married and have children, but the husband dies of a sudden illness. The actors perform the burial very convincingly, crying and wailing and carrying a real coffin around in the village. The husband is barely put to rest before his relatives grab the property and leave the widow and the children to fend for themselves. Our paralegal officer then enters the play to assist the desperate widow.

'Don't worry, the law is on your side. These people are breaking the law. Go to the District Commissioner's office and report this. If he doesn't help you, you can come to our NGO for assistance.'

The woman then goes to the District Commissioner, who refers the case to the chiefs. The paralegal joins the chiefs' sessions and explains the law of inheritance according to which both the widow and the relatives may expect their rightful share. They also explain that anyone who grabs property unlawfully can be fined and even imprisoned, and the matter is resolved with the blessing of the chiefs.

The drama emphasises the primacy of negotiation and mediation. We strongly believe that litigation should be the last resort, because it is so costly in money, time and strained relationships. The drama is then discussed and it works wonders. Property grabbing has reduced considerably in the districts where we work. The paralegals also encourage and assist people in making wills, which is the best safeguard against property grabbing. We provide the forms and help in completing them, and the District Commissioner then has custody of the signed and attested wills.

Our aim is that human rights should be at the fingertips of the people of Malawi and of their judges, chiefs, prison and police officers, politicians and officials, and we are convinced that working with and from the grassroots is the best way to achieve this.

Muluzi's Mbumba

Quite unexpectedly, my principled fight for women's rights occasioned a direct clash with our first democratically elected president, Dr Bakili Muluzi, who defeated Banda in multiparty elections in June 1994. During the dictatorship Dr Banda created the institution of the *Mbumba*. He established himself as the nation's *Nkhoswe*, which according to African tradition is a benign father figure, a family head, who looks after the women and children, clothes them, feeds them and so on. The *Nkhoswe*'s dependants are called the *Mbumba*, and Dr Banda's *Mbumba* was all the women of Malawi. One of the cornerstones of his personal cult was this relationship with the women. He would take care of them and protect them and they would in turn honour and respect him and show their praise, gratitude and deference – through dance.

Dancing is a traditional way of expressing joy in African culture. Among the Ngoni we will dance, for instance, when a lion has been killed. A man-eating animal has been slain by a brave hero and we dance. We dance at weddings and other celebrations and sometimes the women dance alone.

When Dr Banda toured the country and campaigned for our independence people would dance and celebrate before and after the rallies. It was a normal, communal and natural expression of joy and it was fine. Men and women freely joined the dance or sat and watched. It was free and spontaneous. After the Cabinet Crisis, when Dr Banda consolidated his dictatorship, he went too far with this tradition. It became compulsory for his *Mbumba* – that is, the women and not the men – to dance. At every public appearance there was a dance. Women dressed up in the red, green and blue colours of the MCP and wore dresses with Dr Banda's portrait. When he came back from trips abroad it took highly absurd proportions, with huge and extravagant dance events in the National Stadium to honour the return of the *Nkhoswe*. And the women had no choice. Dancing was compulsory. The Young Pioneers would go into the villages and collect women in truck-loads.

'Come on, Banda is coming to address a meeting! Everybody has to come out. Out, out!'

They had to drop everything and leave – their fields, their

UDF women supporters cheering as Bakili Muluzi is sworn in as the
President of Malawi for the second time, June 1999

Courtesy of *The Nation* newspaper

cooking, their children, their husbands – and if a woman refused,
she would be in trouble. If she argued that her husband had
stopped her, he would be arrested and imprisoned.

The good dancers and their leaders were of course rewarded
and Dr Banda would even build a house for an *Mbumba* leader, if he
was especially pleased with her performance and commitment. As
a result women were fighting for these morsels and for the favours
of the *Nkhoswe*. Dr Banda's *Mbumba* was as a tool of pleasure that
dehumanised and humiliated the women of Malawi, and he turned
women into slaves by forcing them to dance for him.

When representatives of civil society, pressure groups,

Churches and officialdom sat down to discuss our Constitution and how to run our country as a multi-party democracy, we explicitly discussed Dr Banda's *Mbumba*. Traditional dancing is of course fully acceptable and an inherent part of our way to celebrate, but we all agreed that nobody should make use of women in that way again.

Slowly but surely, however, Dr Banda's bad habits were taken over by our newly elected politicians. Soon groups of women donned the yellow colours of the new ruling UDF party and gathered to dance wherever President Muluzi turned up. The policy of handouts, which was a fundamental part of Dr Banda's *Mbumba* institution, continued as well, and President Muluzi dished out small amounts of cash to the dancers. It is obvious enough that petty cash thrown around to display the grandeur of the benefactor has no real effect. Women will fight over the money and maybe run out to buy some shampoo. If you want to make a difference to the lives of rural women the support has to be organised and focused. Give them a sum of money that all can share to establish sustainable, income-generating activities, or build them a clinic.

When I realised that the leaders of the opposition had begun to organise women dancers of their own, I felt I had to do something. Malawi CARER issued a series of press releases condemning a number of human rights violations and unacceptable practices. One of these concerned the re-instigation of the *Mbumba* and reasserted the view that it is degrading for women to dance for politicians – politicians in general, that is, and not the President specifically – and that the practice should be stopped as we had all agreed.

Immediately after this, I went to visit our first-born, Nyamazao, in Tanzania. While I was there Nyamazao heard a rumour.

'Mama, I hear that President Bakili Muluzi is saying something against you back home.'

'What can he say against me? I haven't done a thing', I said, but when I returned to Malawi I found that the whole country was up in arms.

Muluzi had interpreted our statement as a personal attack and denounced me in a public rally. According to the press, his speech and his highly rehearsed cheerleaders had sounded more or less like this:

'Since time immemorial people used to dance, where I come from. . . . If a person danced well he or she was appreciated or rewarded for it. Dancing and singing is our tradition. So I wonder why people are asking why Bakili is rewarding dancers? The little God gives me I share with the poor of Malawi!' Here the President waited for the cheering to subside before continuing:

'If you have a problem with that, it is your problem. I am one of the champions of democracy. Were there any NGOs during the MCP era?'

'No, they were not there', the crowd shouted back.

'If there are any NGOs here, they are here because of Bakili Muluzi and the UDF party and the democracy of Malawi. So, do you think somebody can teach me about human rights? Who are you to teach me? No, no! Some people have an agenda of wanting to make women in this country stop dancing!'

'We will not be discouraged', the crowd answered back. 'Send her back to jail!'

'Ladies and gentlemen, do not just copy Western ideas. In this country we have democracy, human rights and respect for women. Yet if you restrict women because of a certain individual. . . '

'It won't happen!' the crowd replied.

'. . . a certain individual, who has received money and wants to advertise in the papers, you will be finished! . . . Singing is part of our culture. Giving each other money in recognition of a good dancer is also our culture. These things you learn in England, that is your own affair. . . . Do not be fooled by people in the name of human rights and do not bring unnecessary things into this country!'

'She is mad! She smokes marijuana!' the crowd booed, and so it went on.

It quickly became top news and the BBC wanted to interview me, but I was still in Tanzania and instead they talked to Lynne Kachere, executive director of the NGO Progressive Women of Malawi. She spoke out very bravely:

'Vera has spoken for all of us. When we were debating this issue right after multi-partyism, President Muluzi was a leading voice in the condemnation of the *Mbumba* practice. It was actually a key part of his campaign to say that Banda was misusing the women of Malawi. Why is he now doing exactly the same thing himself? Vera is right and the Churches are backing this issue as well. We are fighting this war for her.'

I became a little hero and I was very happy for the support of my fellow women activists. After three months the storm settled a bit and I wrote a letter to President Muluzi.

'How can it be', I wrote, 'that I hear you have denounced me? It is even said that you have incited women against me, who have shouted: "Send her back to jail! Who is Vera? Who is this?"

'Let me remind you that when we won the multi-party elections and you were made President, you wanted to make me a minister. You approached me and asked me to become a minister, but I refused. I did not want to become a minister and a part of the government, because I would then be unable to criticise myself.

'After two weeks you came back and asked me to become an ambassador – which was even worse, because I would not only be part of the government but be out of Malawi as well. You called me again and asked me to become a judge, but again I had to tell you that it made no difference. The point is that I want to be able to criticise you people and you agreed: "Yes, Mrs Chirwa, you are right", you said, "we can easily go wrong and we need people like you to point things out for us."

'We agreed and you were publicly supporting the importance of human rights watchdogs wherever you went – even in the Churches. So, Mr President, how can it be that you are denouncing me and inciting the women against me?'

It took him some time to answer my letter, but eventually one of his ministers sent me a reply stating that the whole affair had been grossly exaggerated.

We met shortly after that. The Church was inaugurating a very beautiful building near the airport and President Muluzi was to open it. I was also invited and as usual among the first of the guests to arrive. I strongly disapprove of this concept of 'African time', according to which people arrive terribly late as a rule. I am a lawyer and I always try to be punctual. I took a seat in the hall and waited.

The Banda era has spoiled the mentality of Malawi's ruling elite. When an important person expresses some kind of disapproval of you, the whole 'court', you might say, turns away from you and shuns you – especially the ministers and their wives. Everybody avoided me that day; they isolated me and tried not to sit too close to me. I did not care.

The President and the First Lady came and opened the function and afterwards they took up a position outside, so that people could run over, line up, and shake hands with them. As President Muluzi was getting into his car, he saw me. I was talking to some women and he waved at me. I ignored it, because I thought he was signalling to one of his officials, but he shouted:

'Call the Doctor. I want to greet her!'

I went over and we greeted each other cheerfully to the amazement of the whole entourage.

'We should meet and discuss', he said, and it was a sort of reconciliation between us. I went to see him as Commissioner of the African Commission for Human and Peoples' Rights and we took it from there. We never discussed the issue of the *Mbumba*, but it was my impression that it ended right there at the airport. We shook hands and he showed that he had repented.

10 *Democracy under Threat*

Euphoria is probably the best description of public sentiment after the multi-party elections in June 1994. For the second time in my life our nation had won its freedom and joy, pride and great expectations were savoured quite as hopefully as in the days of independence.

UDF won the elections and defeated Dr Banda with a two-to-one majority. Under President Bakili Muluzi's government Malawians regained their civil and political rights. Malawi's poor international reputation was turned upside down as the new government signed and ratified international human rights instruments and put action behind the commitment to democracy. The national institutional framework was also strengthened and the necessary legal bodies were put in place: the Office of the Ombudsman, the Anti-Corruption Bureau, the Human Rights Commission, the Industrial Relations Courts, the National Compensation Tribunal and so on.

Over night we were free to express ourselves, to assemble, to vote and to stand up for what we believed in. We still try to get used to this new-found freedom, but it is there. Public media are still controlled by the government and critical journalists still risk their health and their lives when they cross blades with powerful politicians and businessmen, but during Dr Banda's time you had to hide in the bush if you wanted a proper conversation. It is not like that anymore. Today we can walk and talk freely on the streets.

The UDF government granted the Malawians their freedom and we should always remember to credit our first democratically elected president Bakili Muluzi for that. It is my impression that President Muluzi was a genuine person, but he was not very well educated and was easily misled. Right after he took office I advised him strongly on this issue:

'Mr President, people will deliberately advise you wrongly to serve their own interests and make you look like a fool. And others are likely to give you bad or faulty information out of ignorance. You should establish a think tank, a little unit of wise people you really trust, which gives you advice from the heart.'

He told me that he had already set up a group of close and trusted advisers. I did not ask who they were, but from the look of how things have gone it truly seems to me that he chose the wrong people.

By the end of his second term in 2004 the economy had declined. Inflation was running wild and ordinary people experienced an unrelenting struggle to survive on their few, hard-earned Kwacha. Food prices had increased and basic living conditions for the majority had undoubtedly deteriorated under the multi-party democracy. Dr Banda had a strong commitment to food security and people did not starve. In contrast, Malawi was tagged on the international map as famine-prone for the first time ever in 2002. For the poor, freedom of expression cannot outweigh the increasing hardships of everyday life, and I understand that it is difficult to appreciate a democracy that leaves you hungrier and more frightened than the dictatorship it was supposed to rectify. People expected democracy to solve their problems. They were promised tangible improvements and those who continue to feel disadvantaged are likely to look back at the Banda era with nostalgia. You cannot eat democracy, and it is sad but understandable that many people feel disillusioned about democracy and human rights when they seem to bring chaos and insecurity.

It is not, of course, a problem of democracy itself, but of our democrats, and the most obvious way in which they fail us is the growing prevalence of corruption. Corruption and nepotism were also part of Dr Banda's system to the extent that they protected his power base, but he would never have allowed the kind of all-pervading, rampant corruption that we experience today. A dictator obviously depends on a strong, efficient state apparatus and Dr Banda would strike fiercely at any public servant or politician who undermined state authority through corruption.

Today corruption has run wild, but politicians only take a stand against it to restore their own credibility. They rattle their swords only when they are forced to step down. They point fingers and claim that they will not take part in the appalling corrupt practices of Malawian politics, but the truth is they are easily bought; they leave their ideals on the doorsteps of ministries when they are invited back into the political game. Malawian politicians are chiefly motivated by personal gain, and we can only work harder to change our political culture.

A President's conduct is a key aspect of any political culture. President Muluzi administered his concern for our people very unconstructively and he took the practice of handing out small amounts of money to its limit. Wherever he went with his entourage, he dished out cash. An important person in African culture – a big man, as we call him – generates his following and establishes his status by supporting his dependants. It is part of our culture to expect a gift from a visiting President, but Muluzi's handouts threatened to become the primary element of Malawi's distributive politics. This is not the right approach in a modern democracy. The state is supposed to distribute the common goods of the nation – build schools and roads, pay our nurses and soldiers

– and support the development of our people in a sustainable and progressive way. The President should symbolise that agenda, even in his private gift-giving shows. Instead Muluzi dished out loose cash without any plan or focus and people got spoiled. They expected this kind of free money without any obligation to make something out of it. The only obligation was to vote for the big man. Consequently, he was always on the move, going from village to village. Instead of sitting down and carefully and thoughtfully running the country, he was busy maintaining his big-man image at huge rallies in the rural areas. The whole exercise became a personal relationship between the President and his dependants, which undercut the people's sense of ownership of and shared responsibility for our democratic state.

Anything that you could call a vision of Malawi's future during Muluzi's rule was primarily a consequence of demands from international donors – but even here things were derailed by a lack of planning and skill on the part of government. The launching of free primary education is a very good example. The UDF government promised free primary education for all, but instead of working it out properly for the benefit our country the initiative was introduced in a rushed and thoughtless way that sought to display the grandeur and resolve of the government and lay hands on maximum funding from the donors. As a result this very important step forward became a chaotic disaster. There were no teachers, no books, and no school structures: children ended up being taught by retired, unqualified teachers under the mango trees. The educational system, strained in the first place, was spread so thinly that the quality declined considerably and the introduction of free primary education became a setback rather than a much-needed improvement.

A democratic government must justify its position by acting in the service of its electors, the people. The ruling politicians are trusted with a responsibility, which in our case they grossly neglect. This is most evident in relation to the UDF government's attitude to our Constitution. When it was ratified our Constitution was considered the best in Southern Africa. We can now attach another and much less flattering ranking to it: one based on the number of times it has been amended. An unscrupulous government has sought to amend it to serve its own ends, and the third term issue was the crudest evidence of this practice to date.

The Third Term

At first we thought it was a joke. Out of the blue one of the UDF ministers publicly stated that the country was faring so well under President Muluzi that he should have a couple more terms. In writing the Constitution we had been very adamant about limiting occupation of the presidency. Section 83(3) clearly prohibited anyone from occupying the office for longer than two consecutive five-year terms. We had had one Life President, and one is more than enough.

Slowly, President Muluzi also started to hint at the third term issue in his speeches:

'Banda did 21 years, but the UDF government will do 30 years!' he would say to a cheering crowd, but people dismissed it as hot air.

Suddenly we realised that they were serious. An Open Term Bill was quickly tabled, which would amend the Constitution and give the President an unlimited number of terms. The government had managed to pull a fast one and the Bill was introduced in Parliament as a private member's Bill by an opposition MP from AFORD. It was rumoured that President Muluzi and the leader of AFORD, Chakufwa Chihana, had begun to meet, and we civil society activists wondered what they were up to. When we found out there was a great uproar. Churches, NGOs and opposition politicians strongly opposed the Bill and AFORD seemed about to split as its members realised that their own party leadership was paving the road for President Muluzi's life presidency.

Unfortunately, but not surprisingly, much of the heated debate became very personal. The third term protagonists were quick to castigate the opposition, which retorted with vitriolic accusations of the rampant corruption in the government. I have always been against this personalisation, which sadly characterises our political discourse, and Ivy and I sat down to write a sober and factual statement on why we opposed the third term. We argued our case from the basis of the Constitution and the principles behind it, to which we had all agreed – including President Muluzi. And we had not even tested the system yet! He was the first President in the Second Republic and we had to see how the system worked before we could consider changing it. The UDF claimed that the President had set so many things in motion, which he now had to follow through. This was of course pure nonsense. If his successor was unable to manage the job, Muluzi was more than welcome to run again after a five-year break.

We sent the statement out through all our channels and had volunteers distributing it to the public in buses and all over. I went to the Parliament in Lilongwe and made its clerk put the statement in the pigeonhole of each and every MP. The civil society organisations and the Churches worked as one and we decided to try and split the President's allies: this led us to approach Dr Banda's old strongman, John Tembo, who had taken over as president of MCP. Tembo was initially supportive of the third term and I think President Muluzi had won him to his side by promising to build the extravagant mausoleum for Dr Banda that Tembo passionately wanted. John Tembo also wanted to become President of Malawi, however, and he had second thoughts as the opposition picked up and the government revealed its intentions of gaining absolute and indefinite power over the country. Tembo and the MCP changed course and joined the opposition, and that was the beginning of the end for Muluzi's dream of a third term.

We were campaigning and praying seriously, and even the Muslims joined the struggle. As a Muslim President Muluzi was generally guaranteed the full support of this minority community, but the third term issue divided them, too, and a number of Muslim leaders opposed the President.

The character and intentions of the UDF government became terrifyingly clear when this stiffening of opposition made them bare their fangs: our fear of experiencing another dictatorship was justified as the government fought back in ways we knew too well. Any hostile discussion of the third term in the public media was suppressed and the country's human rights standing slid lower than at any point since the Banda era. Demonstrations were banned in direct violation of Chapter Four of the Constitution. The police were used as the government's private tool of oppression and sent in to intimidate and break up any opposition assembly. Meanwhile the Young Democrats, the UDF party's youth wing, demonstrated freely in support of the third term and rampaged unhindered like their infamous predecessors, Dr Banda's Young Pioneers. Once again we faced an executive that encouraged political violence, but we were not cowed by the excessive and unlawful use of force. It rather strengthened our resolve. We realised that a line had to be drawn here. Malawi should never be allowed to fall back into dictatorship.

The vote for the Open Term Bill was cast in Parliament. It was a drama. As a people, we held our collective breath. There were rumours that a number of MPs were under pressure to vote for the Open Term Bill but we still hoped that the majority of our legislators would take a stand for constitutional democracy. The Bill was defeated by three votes. Together, we had defended our Constitution.

President Muluzi now called for reconciliation and encouraged all of us to concentrate on rebuilding the country. We thought the storm was over, but before long the Bill was reintroduced. The government itself now tabled a Third Term Bill and claimed that it was quite different from the Open Term Bill, which was untrue. They wanted to press the thing through via a referendum and started to dish out money throughout the rural areas.

My cousins up north saw it at first hand. People were queuing up in front of visiting UDF officials, who handed out cash in return for people's support for a third term.

'I've got my principles', one of my cousins said and turned the money down, but his friends did not hold back.

'Come on, it's free money!' they urged him. And it was.

When the new Bill was discussed in Parliament the government soon realised that they were fighting a losing battle. The MPs had gained courage after the first cliffhanging vote, and even those who had 'eaten' a lot of the government's money fiercely opposed the third term. In order not to lose face completely the government shelved the Third Term Bill by passing it to the Legal Affairs Committee for comment, but the opposition continued to address the issue until it was finally announced that the Bill had been abandoned.

The third term issue was a blessing in disguise for civil society. Our young democracy stood its hardest test and set a precedent for our country. Civil society and the judiciary showed their worth against the guns of the state. In that sense the NGOs came of age, but the parliamentarians also held their ground and we should not forget that it was ultimately in Parliament that the Bill was defeated. For one whole year all our efforts had been channelled into the fight against dictatorship and our limited resources had been diverted from our struggle against poverty and ignorance. We could now resume our work with renewed strength.

'Zinthu Zatani?' was Bakili Muluzi's battle cry when the UDF and the other pressure groups surfaced and rallied the people against Dr Banda in the early 1990s. 'What has happened?'

'Zasintha!' the crowd would respond. 'Things have changed!'

And things have changed. We have won our freedom, but Malawians continue to suffer and fundamental issues like poverty, security, education, health and public morale go from bad to worse. Our political elite has a responsibility, which they not only neglect but also exploit at the expense of our people and we must put our faith in civil society organisations. It took us 30 years to achieve a Malawian democracy. I hope it will not take another 30 years to make Malawian democrats.

Insecurity Brought Home

We are struggling with poverty, mismanagement and corruption – and to make things worse crime has gone up tremendously in recent years. Dr Banda's rule was violent. Dissidents were executed left, right and centre at the whim of the ruling elite, but the violence was monopolised and institutionalised by the regime and ordinary crime was not tolerated. Common people could feel fairly secure if they only supported the system unconditionally and did not stick their heads out.

The level of discipline was also much higher during Dr Banda's regime. The streets were clean and people did not loiter. Beggars and prostitutes were rounded up by the police in large sweeping operations whenever a foreign dignitary visited the country. In prison we couldn't help noticing how they poured in a few days before a state visit.

Now street vendors have taken the law into their own hands in the urban areas. They control the streets completely and any attempt to move them to a designated market area is met with violent demonstrations. President Muluzi saw them as an important voting bloc and a source of potential recruits for his violent

Young Democrats. He just appeased them, which was symptomatic of the way the political leadership of today condones and even breeds this chaotic kind of violence and insecurity.

The general feeling of insecurity also stems from modern forces that tear at our social fabric and threaten the disintegration of our society. In the tourist areas young boys are seduced by older foreign women; they take drugs, drop out of school, and oppose their parents.

When I am addressing the communities, the chiefs and elders always express anxiety and frustration:

'The young people are losing their culture', they complain.

'You have to stand firm on discipline', I tell them. 'You have to ask each and every parent to bring their children up as they themselves were brought up.'

'But the children are very unruly. They say that this is a democracy. They can do what they like.'

'The young people have got it wrong. Unruliness is not democracy! You can move, talk and act freely, but it is very important that other persons' rights are equally respected. Young people have to learn that,' I tell them.

The iron fist of Dr Banda was suffocating the people, but the draconian rule also kept the darker side of public enterprise in check. Today criminals have a free rein. Crime hits you at random and people feel very insecure. One of the first things I noticed when I got out of prison was that walls were being built around our houses. It was not like that before. But I would soon realise how insecure one could feel.

In October 2000, Malawi CARER took up a contested case against an awfully corrupt and unscrupulous minister. The minister had grabbed a poor person's property and the man had been threatened to boot. He came to Malawi CARER and asked the paralegals for help. They wrote to the minister and asked him to return the property or to have an audience with a paralegal and the complainant to discuss the matter. The minister got furious:

'Who does she think she is, this Vera Chirwa? What is Malawi CARER to me? I can go and kill them all', he is reputed to have said. Even the police feared this man.

Two months later my house burned under mysterious circumstances. It was during Christmas and the family had gone to Tanzania to visit Nyamazao, our first-born. She had lost her husband in a plane crash and Zengani, Fumbani and I went to cheer her up a bit. While we were away my watchman called some electricians to fix an electrical problem that had started a small fire in the garage. They detected a fault on the main switchboard, but there was something very fishy about their behaviour and they refused to fix it. The same night a real fire broke out and the house almost burned to the ground. I lost everything I had – including the few photographs, letters and personal items from the time with Orton that I had left after the prison years.

Less than a month after the fire things turned really bad. We had gone to a funeral and returned late in the afternoon. My daughter-in-law, Zengani's wife Makoko, works for Women's Voice. She had just come back from a trip with the Malawian women MPs, who had gone to South Africa to learn from their women colleagues, and she was staying with me in the house. We asked the maids to cook some food for us as we were both quite exhausted. Our gardener suddenly barged into the living room.

'What is it?' I asked, rather irritated.

'I just want to tell you that the dog has eaten all its own cubs', he said.

'Are you bringing this news to me now? Can't you see I'm tired? Tell me tomorrow', I told him, and was a bit puzzled by the situation.

Then another man came in after him. I thought he was accompanying our gardener, but he jumped straight at me.

'Give me your money!', he yelled.

I realised we were being robbed, but I kept calm and even managed to crack a joke.

'But see, we are just coming from a burial and I have no money on me. Why don't you come back on Monday instead?'

It took him a bit off-guard because he just stopped for a second and stared at me before he snapped back into it.

'No, no! We want money now!'

I told them that I had some money in the bedroom. We had a number of alarm buttons in the house, including one in the bedroom, but they knew exactly where it was and pushed me to the ground before I had a chance to activate it.

'Don't let her touch the button', their leader said. They were well prepared for this attack: the dogs did not bark, the guards at the gate had not reacted, and they managed to avoid the alarm system. Someone from the household was obviously involved.

They pushed Makoko and me into the bathroom. There were seven of them and they were raping our two maids in the next room. Two of them pulled down their pants and were about to rape us as well, when their leader called them from the living room.

'Come on, you idiots! Get the money! Get the money first!'

They locked the door and started to loot the house. After a couple of hours they had ransacked everything. They lost the key for the bathroom in the process, and had to smash the door with a big stone to get us out of there.

'Where is your car key?', the leader screamed at me.

'I don't drive', I told him calmly, 'I am being driven and my driver has left.'

They must have managed to find it somewhere or maybe they short-circuited the car. They blindfolded and handcuffed Makoko and me. It reminded me of prison. They dragged us out of the bathroom, threw us into the back of my car and started to pile all my belongings on top of us.

'We're going to cut you if you move. We'll cut off your hands!' they threatened.

'Don't do anything', I cautioned Makoko. 'Just keep praying. Don't try anything. They are not joking.'

Makoko was terrified. I was all right. I am seasoned in that respect. I have been in trouble before, but for Makoko it was the first time of real peril. The poor woman got quite disturbed after that, almost delirious, and I later had to send her home to Zengani, who was working in Namibia, to rest a bit.

The robbers got into the car and drove off with us and the loot, but they had made a mistake. Something set the car's alarm system off and they panicked. We reached two houses down the road before they all jumped out of the car and ran. The gardener, who had let the others in, tried desperately to run off with the television, but he had to drop it. It smashed on the asphalt.

The car had come to a halt outside a neighbouring house and we managed to call the police and the security services by using their alarm system. It was close to midnight.

The two maids gave their statements and we got hold of the head of the women's section of Malawi CARER, Mrs Chisempele, who came and gave them some counselling. One of them slept with me that night and the other slept with Makoko. The next morning Mrs Chisempele took them to the hospital and confirmed that they had been raped. They were tested for HIV/AIDS, but thank God they tested negative.

Within days President Muluzi was swamped by letters from the leaders and congregations of the Presbyterian Church in Canada, Scotland, England and South Africa. They all voiced their concern about the news that I had been attacked and urged him to protect me.

'Vera has suffered in prison for a long time; she should be protected', they wrote, and sent copies to me.

The police managed to catch three of the robbers, but two of them supposedly escaped from custody shortly after their arrest. The one still in custody was my gardener, but he claimed to be innocent. A fourth man was later caught and he revealed everything to the police, including the gardener's involvement. This man was one of the rapists and my maid gave evidence against him in court. They were acquitted, however, despite the cogent evidence. We were shocked. The prosecutor wanted to appeal, but he was immediately transferred up north to a punishment posting far out in the bush.

'I'm being transferred because I insist on appealing this case', he complained, and the whole affair raised a cloud of suspicion: had there been political manipulation? We will probably never know, but one thing is certain: my home no longer felt secure.

Standing for President

When I came out of prison, I was encouraged more or less immediately to stand for President. Dr Banda was still in power and my family feared greatly for my life and did their best to keep me indoors. The first public event of consequence I attended was Chakufwa Chihana's appeal in March 1993 against his conviction on sedition charges at the end of 1992, shortly before my release. I was quickly noticed.

'Vera is here. Vera is here', people whispered and when we left the court house people were cheering.

'Vera! Vera! Vera!'

They wanted me to stand for President and I was being pressed by a group of influential people who wanted to back me. But I was weak and felt it was madness to run for President so soon after 12 years in prison. When nominations were up I deliberately left the country.

At the next presidential elections in 1999, people pushed me even harder, urging me to stand against Muluzi, but I still felt that I was not fully at home in Malawian politics. I really disappointed a lot of supporters, but I decided that I was not yet settled properly after all those years abroad and in prison.

In 2004, I thought the time was ripe. Things were definitely not on the right track in our country. I felt an urge to stand and announced that I was interested in running.

We needed to win this election and get rid of the UDF, and with the help and encouragement of the Churches the opposition parties began to negotiate the formation of a coalition. Such a coalition obviously had to decide on one candidate and the Churches proposed a list of characteristics such a candidate should have and a standard that his or her life should demonstrate. All the opposition leaders jockeyed for that nomination, but I was the only one who satisfied all the conditions laid down by the Churches. I was skilled, experienced, respected and well-known, and I had demonstrated the needed integrity. I stood to win the nomination but I was also a woman, and I am certain that male chauvinism played a major part in the flimsy excuses that were put forward to disregard my offer to lead the opposition. The other opposition leaders failed to agree amongst each other. Gwanda Chakuamba was finally nominated, but John Tembo of MCP and a former UDF strongman, Brown Mpiginjira, who had formed a new party, refused to accept Chakuamba – or rather, their own defeat. A strong, united coalition could not be formed and Muluzi's handpicked successor, Bingu wa Mutharika, who had no popular support, suddenly had a chance in an election that otherwise would have been close to impossible for the UDF even to rig and bully into another win.

There was a call-in programme on Capitol Radio, where the listeners were asked to respond to the idea of having me as their President. We listened very carefully to that programme and decided that the public response was so positive that we should follow it up and do a bit of research in the rural areas. I had a group of people around me who put a lot of energy into this, and they conducted a questionnaire-based survey in a number of key districts to check my chances. It turned out that more than 60 per cent welcomed the idea of me as a candidate for the presidential elections and I was persuaded to try and stand as an independent candidate.

Time was running out for the formal registration as a presidential candidate and the procedure was rather demanding. Twelve people from each district in the country had to sign and vouch for my candidacy and people hurried north and south to complete the forms. They were very well received.

'Oh, how fantastic. We love Mama Chirwa. The men have let us down. Let a woman lead us now. We will of course support her candidacy', people said.

It was very encouraging, but there was a catch.

'Where is the money?' they asked.

For the first time, I really understood the extent to which the UDF had spoiled our people. There I was vigorously debating with them on the phone from Blantyre. The forms were in front of them. They just had to sign.

'Don't you understand that the whole point of my candidacy is to combat corruption?' I asked them.

'Yes, we understand and we fully support you. But we need money. All the candidates pay for their registrations.'

'But how can I run for president, if I start my campaign with a bribe?' I asked and in the end they signed.

However, in one district they refused. I managed to get only two signatures there. The rest insisted on a bribe. I would never pay a bribe to fight corruption and the forms could not be completed. It was also a problem, of course, that I relied on the same constituencies as other opposition candidates and we would have split the vote. In the end I decided not to go through with it and I never formally registered.

Bingu wa Mutharika officially won the election, which I think was rigged. Gwanda Chakuamba disputed the result and for a few days there was violence on the streets. As usual the police used excessive force and ended up shooting an innocent bystander – a little six-year old girl. But the unrest cooled off and, before long, Gwanda Chakuamba joined the UDF government, the latest in a long line of chameleons in Malawian politics.

We have so far been pleasantly surprised by Muluzi's successor, Bingu wa Mutharika. The way he was handpicked by Muluzi and his performance during the election in 2004 made us think of him as nothing but a lapdog and pawn in Muluzi's game to remain in control after his attempt at a third term had failed. It sent shivers down our spine when Mutharika publicly declared that he would never even consider pressing charges against Muluzi, if he was elected President.

His first months in office have left a different picture of our new President. He is busy distancing himself from the corrupt UDF strongmen, who are so furious at being bypassed in ministerial appointments and lucrative government postings that they have begun to whine in public and denounce their new boss. Mutharika has introduced a slim-line Cabinet and crossed blades with Muluzi by holding on to his prerogative to appoint his own team of ministers. We will have to wait and see what happens in our country.

One thing that made me reconsider his potential, is his attitude to dancing. At one of his first large public appearances after taking office truckloads of UDF-clad women were freighted into the venue to dance and cheer for Bingu wa Mutharika. But he refused to give them money and to acknowledge their presence. The women, of course, were disappointed and felt betrayed, and some minor UDF leaders had to run around belatedly and give them a few coins. The press quickly picked up the women's angry remarks and tried to make an issue of it, but Mutharika responded that the practice of dishing out money was over. Women could expect his full support, but in an organised and sustainable way. This issue is very dear to my heart and I am happy that the point I have been arguing all these years has reached the top man at last.

11 *Human Rights Commissioner*

The African Human Rights Commissioners are the torchbearers of human rights in Africa. The Commissioners are appointed on the basis of their integrity, high moral standing and commitment, and I am proud to say that I am one of them. The African Commission on Human and Peoples' Rights convened in November 1987 for the first time. The Commission is a regional human rights body mandated by the African Charter on Human and Peoples' Rights to promote and protect human rights on the African continent. The Commission works to promote human rights through sensitisation of African populations, documentation, and inter-pretation of the principles and rules upon which African governments ought to base their legislation. The primary protect-ive mechanism of the Commission is the communication pro-cedure, which is provided for in the Charter. Individuals, groups or states can submit petitions concerning alleged violations of human rights to the Commission; if these petitions are found eligible, they are then considered by the Commissioners.

The Commission also considers state reports, which are to be submitted every two years by the 53 members states of the African Union (formerly called the Organisation for African Unity), who have all ratified the Charter. The eleven Commissioners are elected for a four-year period by the heads of state of the African Union and meet twice a year for a 15-day session. I was elected in 2001.

Since eleven of us have to cater for 53 member states, we have divided the countries between us. I am responsible for Tanzania,

Uganda, Kenya and Swaziland. Originally a Commissioner was also responsible for his or her own country of residence, but recently this arrangement was changed. We are to discharge our duties without fear or favour, as stated in the Charter, and once we take office we have to be fully independent of our own governments. If a Commissioner is also a trusted member of his or her own government, like an Ambassador or even an Attorney General, as was the case with our Zimbabwean colleague, this independence can be compromised.

Commissioners also undertake missions to monitor serious mass violations of human rights. I have gone to Sierra Leone and Rwanda and still find it hard to digest the atrocities that confronted us on those missions. We can also write resolutions and offer recommendations to the member states in cases of human rights violations. In my time as a Commissioner we have drafted resolutions against Libya, Algeria and Tunisia.

It is widely acknowledged that regional human rights bodies, such as the European, the Inter-American and the African commissions, are of immense importance in promoting progressive implementation of human rights through their case work and their advisory function to member states. The African Commission is so far the only intergovernmental institution that legitimately protects human rights in Africa. Our budget is tight, our meetings and sessions are sometimes postponed or cut short owing to lack of funds, and we receive no salary. Despite the unique and important character of the Commission, funding is terrible. We rely in practice on donors and the African Union totally neglects to live up to its responsibility to enable the Commissioners to discharge their duties. It borders on a disgrace that we are so far from doing what we are supposed to do in terms of missions, fact finding and human rights promotion in our designated countries because funds are lacking. The legal officers in the Secretariat are also badly paid on short-term contracts and the good employees, who give us crucial assistance, often have to seek other jobs to make ends meet.

Yet our work carries weight and Commissioners generally undertake their trusted task with diligence. But there are also many challenges. There is a rift between Anglophone and Francophone Commissioners, for instance, and there is also a tendency for the Muslim Commissioners to form an interest group *vis-à-vis* the others. These minor frictions and misunderstandings can get out of proportion and hinder the progress of our work – our conflicts are sometimes even played out in the public sessions in front of NGOs, donors and government representatives. Because we are supposed to be leaders and examples to follow, I feel very embarrassed to be part of such a dogfight. I have therefore been instrumental in designing a code of conduct for the Commissioners, which will guide us and provide a framework for our interaction and cooperation.

The Whipped Schoolgirls of Sudan

The most recent communication in which I was involved concerned the punishment of eight girl students from Sudan. A group of young men and women from a university in Khartoum went for a picnic along the banks of the Nile. They had sought and obtained permission from the local authorities. Young people do what they do and these students were supposedly flirting and kissing when police and security agents charged the picnic, beat them up and arrested eight of them – all girls. The girls were alleged to have violated public order because they had not been properly dressed and had acted immorally. The girls admitted to having kissed the boys, worn trousers, danced and talked with the boys – and this, according to the local court, was enough to convict and punish them straight away without the presence of a lawyer. The eight girls were sentenced to fines and lashes. The following day each girl received between 25 and 40 lashes on their bare buttocks with a plastic whip that leaves permanent scars.

The girls felt that the punishment was grossly disproportionate. Ordinarily kissing and flirting would not have attracted such grave and humiliating punishment, and they took the case to the African Commission. They argued that they had been victims of cruel, inhuman and degrading punishment as a violation of Article Five of the African Charter.

First of all the Commission had to decide whether the case was admissible: a primary condition is that complainants must have exhausted all domestic remedies for appealing their cases. The girls had appealed with no success and ultimately it was argued that domestic appeal was in any case illusionary, because the punishment was carried out immediately after the verdict. The case was admitted and landed on my desk.

I felt quite strongly about the obvious gender discrimination in this case. Why were the boys not arrested? Apart from the cruel corporal punishment, the psychological humiliation was also a gross violation, when you consider that these young Muslim women were stripped and beaten in public. I ruled that their rights had been violated and recommended that Sudanese criminal law should be amended in conformity with the Charter, that the penalty of lashes should be abolished and that the victims should be compensated. I faced a good deal of oppositional lobbying from my Arab colleagues, but I insisted on these recommendations. The Commissioners offer advice and we have no means of enforcing such recommendations. We depend on the authority of our cause and the goodwill of the member states, but generally our judgements have had effect and have been enforced.

The only petitions from Malawi, to be considered so far are Orton's and mine and Aleke Banda's. In June 1992 Amnesty International petitioned the Commission on our behalf and an appeal on behalf of Aleke Banda, who had been detained in 1980 because of a clash with Dr Banda, was placed before the Commission by his son-in-law. The cases were considered together and the Commission held that four articles of the African Charter had been violated. Before the proceedings were finalised Orton had died and Aleke and I had been released, but the Commission emphasised that the new government of Malawi was responsible for the reparation of the abuses we had undergone.

It seems unlikely that we are the only Malawians who could rightfully seek redress from the Commission, but there is a tremendous information deficit regarding its function and potentials. An action plan has been drawn up to increase general awareness of the Commission and its work, but we have to rely on our small secretariat in Banjul, The Gambia, which has its hands full. The signatories to the Charter must take part in this effort as well, but the government of Malawi has not bothered to inform the public about the Commission and how to access it. I have tried my best to raise funds from donors to hold a series of workshops and seminars for government officials, chiefs, universities, schools and grassroots organisations. I have received a lot of sympathy but no financial commitment and I can only push things a little further forward on my own. Every time I return from the biannual sessions I call a press conference and report on the Commission's work. I have lately been very vocal about our government's failure to submit the biennial state reports by which the government declares Malawi's human rights status. Malawi has not reported to the Commission since 1994 and has gravely neglected its obligations as a signatory to the Charter. Commissioners' work as human rights watchdogs is hindered by such an unwillingness, since they are supposed to intervene in a negative human rights situation on the basis of this reporting. In the long run, however, this will rebound on the Malawian government and the many other African member states that fail to report. When all means to obtain reports have been exhausted the Commission's last alternative is to delegate human rights NGOs to submit reports on the government's behalf – and they may make scathing reports that paint a very negative picture of the human rights situation in the defaulting country.

Special Rapporteur on Prisons

The Commission also has a Rapporteur system, where certain Commissioners are appointed to monitor a specific field of high importance in the promotion and protection of human rights on the continent. We have Special Rapporteurs on Women, Arbitrary Killings, Human Rights Defenders, and Prisons. I know prisons from the inside. I have seen and experienced the suffering and I care for people in prisons. I really have a heartfelt calling to improve prison conditions in Africa and I was more than pleased when my colleagues in the Commission insisted on making me the Special Rapporteur on Prisons.

Prison conditions in Africa – food, accommodation, treatment, facilities, legal protection, everything – are terrible, and there is a profound need to revolutionise the whole penal system. The ridiculously poor African nations cannot afford to give each and every prisoner bacon and eggs for breakfast, of course, but an absolute minimum standard must be upheld. There is absolutely no excuse for sinking below such a standard, but reaching it in the first place is a tremendous challenge. A prisoner should have palatable food in sufficient quantity, a humane place to sleep, and the wherewithal to keep himself or herself clean. For many prisoners these fundamental requirements are something they can only dream of – and we are not even talking about visits, medical attention, counselling, education, vocational training and the other facilities a prison institution is supposed to provide.

As a Special Rapporteur I visit member states on request or out of my own interest and concern. I have visited Mozambique, Uganda, Namibia, Niger, Benin and South Africa. Many other countries have requested me to come, but the funding is limited. Up to now Penal Reform International has funded the Rapporteur on Prisons, but recently this organisation has made dramatic cutbacks and I am at a loss as to how I can fulfil my duties in the future.

Special Rapporteurs offer their findings and recommendations to the Head of State after a visit and it might seem strange that prison services with immense human rights problems should request a visit from a human rights watchdog. However, my approach to this job is not to criticise, blame or find faults. I see it as my duty to help and encourage the prison services to improve. I am also very conscious of addressing the problems and concerns of both prisoners and staff. To the prisoners, for instance, I would say:

'We have seen how dirty the kitchen and toilets are. And we can see how dirty you are! You have a responsibility here. You have a part to play. Don't expect the officers to do things for you. Clean your things and live under clean conditions. Cook your food properly and look after yourselves. Help the officers help you.'

I would then turn to the officers, 'You are officers and bearers of your government's responsibilities. You have a duty to give these people soap and proper food. It's up to them to clean and cook under hygienic conditions, but you have to cater for them. It's your duty to treat them well. They are human beings. If you treat them like animals they will retaliate and become nasty. If you treat them like human beings, they become human beings. You need to cooperate.'

I strive to consider both sides and I encourage prisoners to take responsibility: 'The prison officers can be your friends!' I tell them. 'Don't be nasty to them. If you're sentenced to hard labour,

Vera Chirwa (centre), in her capacity as Special Rapporteur of Prisons, tasting prison food at Chicheri Prison, August 2003

Courtesy of *The Nation* newspaper

do the labour and cooperate.' And I insist that prisoners and staff have a mutual interest in putting things right and improving the life they share day after day. They like that and I love this work. It is hard, but rewarding.

I have of course visited many Malawian prisons in my capacity as Special Rapporteur but also in connection with the prison reform projects of Malawi CARER. Paralegals from Malawi CARER have trained and informed prisoners and staff about human rights in prison and have started legal aid clinics in the country's four major prisons. The legal aid input involves educating prisoners in basic law procedures and rules applicable to their given situation. The paralegals also follow prisoners to court and assist the court, the police and prison services in expediting cases – especially those involving vulnerable groups such as juveniles, women, and mentally and terminally ill prisoners.

Recently, I have seen a positive change in Malawian prisons, but at one point prisoners were worse off than during Dr Banda's regime. Authoritarian rule under Dr Banda entailed a level of order and control. You were given two blankets, for instance, the first day you arrived in prison. Each year you were imprisoned you received another blanket. I think I had about twelve when I was released: some served as a mattress, others as pillows. In that way Dr Banda was catering for the prisoners. We also had proper uniforms and utensils.

When I visited Zomba Prison a few years after my release the prisoners showed me the torn blankets from the Banda years, ragged uniforms and plates that had nearly rusted away.

'Look Mama', they complained. 'How can we sleep in this? How can we eat from these plates?'

I immediately held a press conference and asked for an appointment with President Muluzi. As a Rapporteur I always try to see the top man directly, instead of trying to push a message up through the ranks of the prison service.

President Muluzi was a bit shocked that I had told the press that prison conditions in Malawi were the worst in Africa. I had only been Special Rapporteur for a short period and have since then seen worse, but I must admit that Zomba Prison made a very bad impression on me at that time. I reported to President Muluzi in detail and he was quite moved. As we wrapped up the meeting I challenged him on an old promise he had given me:

'By the way Mr President. Do you remember that you once told me that I should take you to a prison one day? You still owe me that visit.'

'Ah, yes, I have not forgotten that promise, but you know when I want to go and see people I must have something to offer them, and I have not had the money for such a visit yet. But now I'm all right. Let us go to Zomba Prison together so I can see things for myself.'

He did his best and brought two lorries of things – bread, sugar, buckets and plates. The prisoners were in awe, but they were proud and happy to have been paid a visit by President Muluzi himself. He went to Chichiri Prison as well and brought the prisoners there blankets. Conditions have improved since then. Things change little by little.

12 *The Power to Forgive*

We raised a stone on Orton's grave. It was very sad for me not to have attended the actual funeral, but we formally unveiled the stone at a public ceremony in 1995. The children came and it was the first time I saw them all together. President Muluzi was the guest of honour. He was newly elected and made a lot of promises that day.

Truth and Reconciliation?

When Orton escaped, Banda's Young Pioneers razed his ancestral community to the ground. The Pioneers went into a frenzy and smashed the whole village – burnt the houses, destroyed the crops, and cut down the fruit and coffee trees.

The community never really recovered from that destruction and President Muluzi now promised to set the record straight and rebuild the school to honour Orton's dedication to education and rural development. He also promised to construct a road and a bridge to ensure public access to Orton's grave. In fact, he was quite displeased with the grave:

'Mrs Chirwa, this is not a suitable grave for a national hero', he complained.

'Well, Mr President, it is what his sons and daughters can afford', I told him.

'Oh, but this won't do. I will send a research mission to Zimbabwe to visit the monuments they have built for their freedom fighters. I want Mr Chirwa to have a proper grave!'

Nothing ever happened, but President Muluzi also ran from a much more important promise. At the ceremony he stressed his commitment to get to the bottom of things regarding Orton's death. He used the opportunity to castigate the MCP as a criminal party with a dreadful past and he gave his personal guarantee that a Commission of Inquiry would look into Orton's death.

The inquiry was discussed in the papers. The problem with our political discussion is the personal denunciation and castigation of opponents that becomes the driving force of any debate. It generates a very unfruitful and divisive political climate, and the discussion of Orton's inquiry was no exception. President Muluzi continued to attack MCP leader John Tembo personally and public sympathy almost shifted in Tembo's favour. More importantly, Dr Banda's old strongman hit back, landing his blows where President Muluzi was most vulnerable:

'He might claim that we are criminals', Tembo stated in the papers, 'but who was secretary general of MCP when the Chirwas were arrested? It was no other than President Muluzi himself! How can he point a finger?'

There is a rumour that Bakili Muluzi had boasted that he was going to give Dr Banda a very special Christmas present in 1981, and that, as secretary general of MCP at that time, he played a role in our abduction. Muluzi fell out with Dr Banda shortly after and I do not know or care about the truth in this. The bottom line is that the inquiry into Orton's death was shelved. A more serious obstacle to the inquiry than Muluzi's and Tembo's dogfight was probably that many were calling for a comprehensive inquiry into *all* political murders. People also wanted the infamous Mwanza killings and the murders of other high-profile dissidents looked into. A growing public demand of this nature is likely to have scared the old political hands, which still rule our country, into a silent agreement across the political divides not to open Pandora's box.

We have not had a truth and reconciliation process to heal our wounds as a people after the Banda years. Knowing the truth, and knowing that the truth was known, would have done much for the victims and the surviving relatives. They would have reconciled themselves. We would also have had an opportunity to clean the slate. The politicians of today, on both sides, are with very few exceptions old dinosaurs from the Banda era. They have all been involved in the autocracy and continue to influence Malawian politics with their old conflicts and their undemocratic ways.

Ivy, Kathryn and I tried to document victims' destinies when we were at the Legal Resource Centre and later at Malawi CARER. We issued a press release and people started to come to us and tell their stories. By coincidence I learned something quite significant about our abduction. One of the victims narrated the story of his father's death.

'My father was taken from the house. I'm sure that the man who called himself Mwananku was responsible. He did a lot of harm. I never saw my father again.'

When I heard his story the name puzzled me: 'Mwananku, Mwananku . . . where have I heard that before?' And then it struck me: Mwananku was the man who had invited Orton to the MAFREMO meeting in 1981 and taken us for that fatal drive into the night. Apparently he had the misery of other victims and survivors on his conscience. Later I heard from others that he had been a government agent and had had a hand in the murder of Mkwapatira Muhango as well. Muhango was the publicity secretary of MAFREMO: his house in Zambia was torched shortly after our abduction. Muhango and his entire family perished in the fire.

I wanted to see him. I wanted to find out what had happened and to discover the truth about it all. He lived just down the road in Blantyre, but my family was very afraid.

'Oh, this Mwananku is very dangerous. He'll kill you, Mama. He is ruthless!' And they insisted that I should keep a distance between myself and this man. Eventually he died and I never met him again.

Information about what happened to you is important for victims like myself. When the circumstances of your loss are disclosed and recognised, you are able to console yourself and settle down with your grief. We should have had that opportunity as a nation, but it has not happened yet. Many were thrown to the crocodiles in Shire River and whole groups of people like the Jehova's Witnesses were killed and persecuted. I do not think that taking those who may have been responsible to court is the right thing to do today. You could argue that Dr Banda should have been tried, but time has passed and we need to move on. However, knowing the truth would lengthen peoples' memories, so to speak. We would cherish our democracy more and feel less inclined to think back on the Banda era with nostalgia. People might not want the old perpetrators to run our country if we had a truth and reconciliation process.

The Power to Forgive

When our death sentence had been confirmed and we drove from the Court House. Orton and I promised each other to forgive.

'Let's forgive them all, Vera', he told me. 'Maybe they didn't know what they were doing, maybe they were afraid and couldn't do anything else. Let's even forgive Banda.'

'I've already forgiven them', I said and this has been my strength. That drive and the promise we made to each other on the road from the court to Zomba Prison, where we were to suffer for many years, was a key moment in my life.

After my release many journalists have quizzed me about my

relationship to Dr Banda. I remember the first interview I gave to a foreign woman journalist.

'Suppose Banda says: "Come to State House", will you go, Mrs Chirwa?' she asked.

'No, I won't go, because I don't know what would happen. I might have forgiven him, but he might not accept my forgiveness, and anything could happen then.'

'Then suppose he came to your doorstep. Would you allow him in?'

'Yes, I would let him in. I have forgiven him.'

'How can you forgive a man who has done so much harm to you?' she asked, and people – especially Westerners – generally find it hard to understand. I suppose it is because I am a Christian.

The most fundamental thing to realise as a human being is the importance of loving your neighbour. You should not love the Bible, but love the profoundly good social ideas it talks about. According to my understanding you can also base your promotion of human rights on Christianity. If you want to build a happy society people need to love each other and if they love each other they will not violate each other's rights. Love your neighbour and do not violate your neighbour's rights. According to me it all boils down to this love. Love your neighbour – that is all.

My ability to forgive comes from that love. And it does not matter to me whether those who have wronged me have repented or not. I forgive. I have scared quite a few people with this capacity of mine.

Both Chief Nazombe and Chief Mzukuzuku, who presided over our cases in the traditional court and the appeal hearing that followed, were my father's relatives. Chief Nazombe, whose court sentenced us to death, is still alive and after my release he did his best to avoid me. At a large church ceremony up north in Livingstonia, we bumped into each other. He was with a good friend of mine, Chief Mzikubola, who came to greet me. Nazombe was

Vera Chirwa with her old friends David and Gertrude Rubadiri,
December 2003

caught unawares and did not have time to run away.

'Hello, how are you?' I said and stretched out my hand.

He accepted it, but he was visibly shaken. Later I was chairing
a meeting in Blantyre that he attended, and I offered him the floor.
He was very happy and praised me highly. As a wronged person
you have that ability to break the barrier and show that your
forgiveness is genuine. I have even shaken hands with John Tembo.
I do not know whether it moved him as it has moved many others,
but it does not matter to me. I have forgiven them.

'Forget it. Don't fear me. Everything is okay. Those were
difficult times. What could you do.'

I manage to get that message across and it really affects people.
Chief Nazombe and I have become friends.

I even ran into Mr Chikwenembe, the senior officer who had chained me and mistreated Orton and me gravely. Our eyes accidentally met at the Post Office in Blantyre and he quickly looked away. I marched over and greeted him. He jumped. I do not think he slept that night.

I have also met some of the women guards, who were particularly nasty to me:

'Don't worry', I told them, 'I have no grudge against you. It was the system under Banda and his government. That's all. Let's be here together now. Let's love each other.'

When Dr Banda was dying I went to see him. He was in his deathbed in the Adventist Hospital in Blantyre. Kadzamira was there.

'Hello, Mama, how are you?' she greeted me.

'I'm fine. I have come to see the old man', I told her.

He was sleeping. Kadzamira told me about Dr Banda's condition and wanted to wake him up.

'Oh, no, it's fine. Let him sleep. I'll just sit here for a short while', I said.

Kadzamira stepped aside and I sat by his bed. The Lion of Malawi – our old family doctor, the liberator of our nation, the ruthless dictator who had killed my husband and made me suffer so much.

'Here lies a great man', I thought.

Orton and I had admired many of Dr Banda's qualities as a leader. He was a fantastic administrator and he conducted his affairs properly. But he was cruel, very cruel. His hunger for power created a reign of terror and he was indeed a lion in so far as people feared him like one. He was so tough that we thought he would never die. At that point I even doubted that he would finally pass away. I still thought he would recover.

'I have no time to be sick', he always said. 'I have no time to die.' And when the ministers opposed him he swore – as in a spell or a curse – to outlive them all. But the lion was helpless now and

I felt pity for him. I prayed for him and said goodbye.

A long time ago, Orton and I had fought side by side with this man, but more recently we had fought against him. Our fight had been a fight for justice and prosperity for our people. We fought for the right to express ourselves, to assemble peacefully, to write and print our opinions, to worship the God of our choosing. We fought for personal security, the right to be free from unlawful arrest and unreasonable detention. We fought for the freedom to move inside and outside our nation. We fought to live free from the fear created by an oppressive and intolerant government. We fought to give voice to the many Malawians who remain marginalised and disempowered. We fought to empower women to participate in all aspects of Malawian society. We fought for the rights of children, the rights of prisoners, and more recently the right of those affected by the HIV/AIDS scourge. We fought for the right to development and economic equality. We fought for an accountable and transparent government that is accessible and responsive to an electorate.

Orton and I fought together. He died fighting. And I fight on.

Afterword

Morten Kjærum
DANISH INSTITUTE FOR HUMAN RIGHTS

How can one describe Vera Chirwa's remarkable biography? As an historical record it works on two levels: on the one hand it offers us a unique insight into the Malawian struggle for independence from British rule during the 1950s, full of crystal-sharp detail and unforgettable events, and on the other hand it functions as a universal saga depicting the twentieth-century battle against colonialism and institutional racism that took place across the globe during those tumultuous years.

The same applies to Vera's own individual story. As a member of the first generation of Africans to become lawyers and human rights activists, she is a unique figure in Malawian history, a woman who was prepared to sacrifice everything to win justice and freedom for her people. But she also writes movingly about being a mother, and about the sacrifices she and her family had to make to achieve this higher goal. In that sense this story is also about the ordinariness of being a mother and wife and some of the most poignant scenes in the book describe incidents where everyday concerns clash with the higher ideals to which both Vera and her husband dedicated their lives.

Above all else, the book is a dramatic record of the indomitable spirit of a woman who refused to accept things as they were. We follow her personal struggle against injustice from the age of five when she is severely beaten by her father for refusing to do her chores and runs away from home, to the time when she and her husband are sentenced to death by a kangaroo court. And the story does not end there. As she says on the last page, 'I fight on'.

Apart from Vera's extraordinary tenacity and dedication, what shines through this book is her capacity to forgive her enemies. Despite years of incarceration in filthy prison cells, despite all the privations inflicted on her family, Vera never sounds bitter. Her story is an inspiration to all human rights activists who strive to achieve justice even when the odds seem to be hopelessly stacked against them. It proves that fortitude and strength of purpose can topple oppressive regimes and help to create a more just society. Vera Chirwa's story personifies this struggle for justice and the rule of law, for democracy and rights for all – for Africans and other colonised people, for women and prisoners, and for all disadvantaged, marginalised and vulnerable persons. Vera Chirwa fought at great risk and cost and with courage and compassion against such diverse incarnations of human rights offenders as the British Empire, Malawi's one-party dictatorship during the Cold War, and the country's young, predatory post-colonial democracy.

It has been an honor for the Danish Institute for Human Rights to support this book project from the beginning. Like the stories of other champions of the war against injustice and oppression, such as that of Mahatma Gandhi and Nelson Mandela, Vera Chirwa's biography deserves to be passed on to future generations.

Morten Kjærum
DIRECTOR OF THE DANISH INSTITUTE FOR HUMAN RIGHTS, AND MEMBER OF
THE UN COMMITTEE ON THE ELIMINATION OF RACIAL DISCRIMINATION
Copenhagen 2007

Index